# AFRICA

## The Struggle for Independence

**WORLD HISTORY LIBRARY**

# AFRICA

## The Struggle for Independence

DENNIS WEPMAN

Facts On File

*On the cover: Dakar*, by Hardy Botha (from *Resistance Art in South Africa*, © 1989, Sue Williamson; courtesy of David Philip Publishers, Ltd.) In *Dakar*, South African artist Hardy Botha depicts a 1987 meeting in Dakar, Senegal, between the outlawed African National Congress and a largely Afrikaans-speaking South African delegation, including Botha. The meeting resulted in a joint communique, supporting a negotiated settlement for South Africa, a call for the release of all political prisoners, and the lifting of the ban on the ANC.

**Africa: The Struggle for Independence**

Copyright © 1993 by Dennis Wepman

Facts On File, Inc.
460 Park Avenue South
New York, NY 10016

**Library of Congress Cataloging-in-Publication Data**
Wepman, Dennis.
    Africa: the struggle for independence / Dennis Wepman.
        p.   cm. — (World history library)
    Includes bibliographical references and index.
    ISBN 0-8160-2820-6
    1. Africa—History—Juvenile literature.   2. Africa—History—
    Autonomous and independence movements—Juvenile literature.
    I. Title.   II. Series.
DT22.W47   1993
    960—dc20                    93-20020

A British CIP catalogue record for this book is available from the British Library.

Facts On File books are available at special discounts when purchased in bulk quantities for businesses, associations, institutions, or sales promotions. Please contact our Special Sales Department in New York at 212/683-2244 or 800/322-8755.

Text design by Donna Sinisgalli
Cover design by Amy Beth Gonzalez
Composition by Facts On File, Inc./Robert Yaffe
Manufactured by the Maple-Vail Book Manufacturing Group
Printed in the United States of America

10 9 8 7 6 5 4 3 2 1

This book is printed on acid-free paper.

# CONTENTS

*Over 200 million of our people cry out with one voice of tremendous power—and what do they say? We do not ask for death for our oppressors, we do not pronounce wishes of ill-fate for our slave masters, we make an assertion of a just and positive demand. Our voice booms across the oceans and mountains, it calls for freedom for Africa. Africa wants her freedom. Africa must be free. . . .*

*For years Africa has been the footstool of colonialism and imperialism, exploitation and degradation. . . . Her sons languished in the chains of slavery and humiliation, and African exploiters and self-appointed controllers of her destiny strode across her land with incredible inhumanity, without mercy, without shame, without honour. These days are gone for ever and now I, an African, stand before this august Assembly of the United Nations and shall speak with the voice of freedom proclaiming to the world the dawn of a new era.*

—Kwame Nkrumah, Ghana, address to the
General Assembly of the United Nations, 1961,
quoted by David Rooney, *Kwame Nkrumah*
(New York: St. Martin's Press, 1988), p. 181

# EARLY GLORIES

Here gold is found in great abundance, and huge elephants,
and ebony, and all sorts of trees growing wild. The men, too,
are the tallest in the world, the best looking, and the longest
lived.

> —Herodotus, c. 450 B.C., writing of the land of
> Kush

Untangling the history of Africa, as one modern
scholar has complained, is like trying to trap wind in a net. The second
largest continent after Asia, Africa is more than three times the size of
the United States, and its nearly 12 million square miles cover almost
20 percent of the earth's surface. It is peopled by many races, speaking
more than 1,000 distinct languages and now occupying over 50 independent nations. And its history stretches back before that of any other
region in the world.

Most scientists agree that it was on the African continent that the
human race originated. Fossil remains found in 1959 in Olduvai Gorge
(in what is now Tanzania) include, not only the bones of human beings
some 2.5 million years old, but the first evidence of tool-making—one
of the elements that distinguishes humankind from other animals.
More important yet, these same remains indicate the beginnings of
social life. Signs of cooperation in hunting, the sharing of food, and the

establishment of campsites show that in Africa the human race took its first steps toward civilization.

The roots of independence go very deep in African history. The continent called "the mother of mankind" was to be the cradle of many great independent nations over the thousands of years that followed.

## EGYPT

The people north of the Sahara, that vast desert that stretches from the Atlantic Ocean to the Red Sea in the northern third of the continent, were the first to establish a complex, organized society in Africa. As the water levels of the rivers and lakes in the upper Nile Valley began to rise, about 11,000 years ago, the people living there were able to find rich sources of fish and other food. They no longer had to depend on wild vegetables and game to survive, and they began to form semipermanent settlements. As early as the seventh century B.C., 9,000 years ago, settlers in North Africa were herding oxen and cultivating several varieties of barley and wheat. In time, these extended settlements grew into cities.

The first of the great urban civilizations in Africa was Egypt, which still exists today. Egypt grew up along the Nile River and was a link between western Asia and the rest of Africa. Seven thousand years ago Egypt was already growing into a nation, with good-sized cities built of brick. Farmers irrigated the land, and skilled artists carved stone, wood, and ivory. Gold and silver were mined for jewelry, copper was smelted for tools and weapons, and trade flourished between villages.

Historians usually date the founding of the nation at around 3200 B.C., when the first king of a unified Egypt established a government over the whole country and passed his rule down to his son. A series of kings and queens of the same family is called a dynasty, and in its nearly 3,000 years of independence, ancient Egypt had 30 dynasties. The nation grew into a powerful empire with foreign provinces stretching thousands of miles, from Ethiopia, deep in the interior of the continent, to modern-day Turkey in Asia Minor.

The culture of ancient Egypt was a highly developed one. The people created an elaborate religion and a complex social system with

*Two great monuments of ancient Egyptian art: the Sphinx and the Great Pyramids.*
(Courtesy of the New York Public Library Picture Collection)

specialists educated in various crafts and professions. Egyptians developed a system of writing and a very accurate calendar and maintained great centers of learning. They used geometry to construct canals and irrigation ditches, and their achievements in architecture and engineering still amaze us. They erected huge statues and vast stone temples that required advanced technical knowledge. The Great Pyramid at Giza, constructed about 2600 B.C., is more than a half-mile around at the base and towers to 450 feet in height. No less impressive is the sophistication of Egyptian art, from such huge stone figures as the Sphinx to the expert paintings that decorated the walls of their palaces and tombs and the exquisitely wrought jewelry of their nobles.

Around 1100 B.C., the empire began to grow weaker. Foreign invaders stripped it of many of its provinces and finally reached the borders of Egypt itself. When Alexander of Macedon conquered Egypt in 332 B.C., native rule ended, and Africa had perhaps its first taste of colonization. More than 2,000 years were to pass before the continent was to see the last of it.

## KINGDOMS IN EAST AFRICA

The Sahara was a great natural barrier. Its 3.5 million square miles made trade difficult between Egypt and the rest of Africa except along the fertile strip bordering the Nile. Nevertheless nations throughout the continent maintained contact in ancient times, and Egyptian trade below the desert flourished for over 2,000 years. One major sub-Saharan nation to develop in the east was the kingdom of Kush, mentioned in the Bible, which began around 2000 B.C. as an Egyptian city along the Nile. By 700 B.C., Kush was large and powerful enough to revolt against the mother country and establish its independence. Africa's first great inland empire, Kush prospered for over 1,000 years, outliving the Egyptian empire from which it sprang.

Further south, the kingdom of Axum, the ancestor of contemporary Ethiopia, began in the first years of the Christian era and remained a powerful nation for 600 years. Below the Zambesi River, the kings of Zimbabwe ruled over an area that covers the present-day republic of that name as well as part of modern Mozambique. The kingdom originated during the fifth century and lasted until the 16th. Little is known of its history, but it left some of the most impressive architecture on the continent. A huge ruin called Great Zimbabwe, probably dating from the 16th century, has stone walls 32 feet high and 20 feet thick.

## KINGDOMS IN WEST AFRICA

Not all the great early societies on the continent grew up in the east. The first of the important West African kingdoms was Ghana, founded in the fifth century north and west of the present-day nation that took its name. Fabled for its splendor, the ancient kingdom boasted cities of as many as 30,000 people, and its royal palace had windows made of glass centuries before that luxury was known in Europe. In the early 1200s, the empire of Mali (in the same area as the modern country but almost twice as large) absorbed Ghana. However, internal struggles so weakened Mali that it was conquered and made a part of the Songhai empire in the 16th century. The powerful Songhais in turn were to fall to Moroccan invaders less than a hundred years later.

This succession of West African kingdoms included some of the most highly advanced cities of their time. Timbuktu, founded around 800 in what is now Mali, was a great international trading center through which passed much of the world's ivory, silk, and gold. Famed as a cultural center, it was described by an Arab traveler in 1550 as containing "numerous judges, doctors, and clerics, all appointed by and receiving good salaries from the king . . . There is a big demand for books and manuscripts. More profit is made from the book trade than from any other line of business."

Throughout Africa there are evidences of former glories. From the highly refined rock paintings in the Sahara's Tassili plateau—a record of human and animal life going back 8,000 years—to the majestic bronze castings of medieval Ashanti and Benin, the continent reveals a long, diverse, and elaborate tradition in art. Its political, social, and intellectual life has been no less developed.

For centuries, Europeans who visited Africa saw it as "the dark continent," a wild and primitive place with no political or legal system of its own. Thus they felt justified in taking the land to bring order and civilization to it. But those who know Africa know that over the thousands of years of its history it has had governments as organized and stable, and laws as clearly defined, as any in Europe or Asia. And if the diverse styles of life were different from those of outsiders, they were often no less civilized. An English historian, writing of African societies of the ninth and 10th centuries, observed,

> Africans, who eventually spoke more than a thousand different tongues, had almost as many systems of behavior and belief. Some of these systems produced societies whose standard of living—in terms of food, personal safety and freedom—equaled that of contemporary societies in Europe. In some instances they were even more advanced: African societies practiced a simple but effective social welfare in their concern for widows and orphaned children.

With such historic traditions, the peoples of Africa found colonization by foreign powers especially bitter. It is not surprising that

## THE KINGDOM OF GHANA

Ancient Ghana was the first major kingdom in West Africa. The present nation of Ghana took its name from this great land when it won its independence from Great Britain in 1957, although it occupies a much smaller territory south and east of the earlier nation. The ancient kingdom included much of today's Mauritania, Guinea, Senegal, Gambia, Mali, Burkina Faso, and Sierra Leone.

Settled by the ancestors of today's Soninke people, Ghana was probably established around the year A.D. 400 as a route for trade between North Africa and the continent below the Sahara. By the year 1000, when Europe was just beginning to emerge from the Dark Ages, Ghana had already grown into a large and powerful kingdom. An Italian traveler of the time described Ghanaian banquets "more lavish than any man had ever seen before" at which lords fed thousands of people at one time. The cities of Ghana rivaled Rome, Paris, and London in both size and luxury. Its capital, Kumbi Seleh, 200 miles north of Bamako in present-day Mali, became the chief market and the cultural center of West Africa. There were artists and scholars at the court, which was famous for its splendor, and the city had paved roads and a highly efficient system of sanitation. The government of Ghana had a well-organized legal system and a national budget for education.

they fought back to reclaim their homes. The many free and powerful kingdoms that had grown up throughout the continent for centuries left a legacy of pride and independence that made resistance inevitable.

### CHAPTER ONE NOTES

p. 1     "Here gold is found . . ." Herodotus (c. 450 B.C.), quoted in Basil Davidson. *Africa in History* (New York: Macmillan, 1974), p. 29.

The most important merchandise that passed through Ghana was gold, carried from West Africa to the Mediterranean cities, and salt, transported south in great camel caravans. The kingdom grew rich as a way station, taxing the goods that passed through the country and finally controlling the market in both of these precious minerals. The gold of Ghana was the finest in the known world.

The Soninke were the lords of Ghana, but other peoples lived in the region, and so the kingdom grew to an empire, dominating the entire region of West Africa. In time its wealth became so great that the kingdoms it traded with were tempted to invade it. The Berbers, a Muslim tribe that had conquered and colonized North Africa around A.D. 700, began raiding the rich Ghanaians. In 1076 the Muslims declared a holy war against Ghana and attacked the kingdom. They captured Kumbi Seleh, plundering its treasures, taxing the citizens, and forcing many to become Muslims. These Berbers did not destroy the kingdom, but they weakened it greatly. Soon other neighboring tribes were able to take advantage of the situation, and what remained of the empire came under attack from every side. In 1230, the last important Ghanaian city fell, and the royal government was unable to maintain control over the land. The once-mighty empire, which had flourished for over 500 years, split into many small states, each with its own ruler.

p. 5    "Numerous judges, doctors, and clerics . . ." Leo Africanus, *Description of Africa* (1550), quoted in Milton Jay Belasco and Harold Hammond. *Africa: History, Culture, People* (New York: Cambridge Book Co. 1981), p. 39.

p. 5    "Africans, who eventually spoke . . ." Basil Davidson. *African Kingdoms* (New York: Time-Life Books, 1966), p. 21.

# THE COMING OF THE EUROPEANS

Kenya would be a paradise if the Europeans went back
where they came from. Don't think I don't like the English.
I do like them—in England. Where they will soon be.
              —Jomo Kenyatta

North Africa had been an important link between
Europe and the Near East since ancient times, but it was not until the
1400s that the first European ships began to arrive south of the Sahara.
Drawn by the fabled wealth of the continent—two-thirds of the world's
gold came from sub-Saharan West Africa in the Middle Ages—and by
the desire for easier trade routes to Asia, European adventurers made
many unsuccessful efforts to enter the continent from the west before
improvements in the science of navigation made the journey possible.

## THE OPENING OF THE CONTINENT

The voyage from Europe to Africa below the Sahara was a perilous one.
The seas were stormy, there were few safe harbors, and the land was
vast and unmapped. But in the early 1400s, it finally became possible
to reach Africa by an Atlantic route. The first to reach the coast were

the Portuguese, a seafaring people who depended on foreign trade to survive. The brother of the Portuguese king, Prince Henry "the Navigator," was so eager to promote his country's expeditions that he set up special training schools for sailors. By the 1470s, Portuguese ships had not only found their way to the gold fields of West Africa but built prosperous trading posts there and forts to protect them from both the native population and rival European traders. Soon Portuguese adventurers established permanent settlements in Africa and developed their own gold mines. In the 1480s they discovered two uninhabited islands they called Príncipe and São Tomé (now politically linked as a single independent republic, off the coast of Gabon). There they cultivated sugar plantations, worked by Africans. In the 16th century, these prosperous plantations were the main source of sugar for all of Europe.

Although the Portuguese tried to keep control of all the businesses they developed, other European countries soon began to compete. During the next few centuries, England, France, Denmark, and the Netherlands entered the field. They traded for gold, ivory, and cloth along the West African coast, and they too built forts to protect their trading posts. In 1652, the Dutch built a settlement in what is now South Africa and expanded it into a large, powerful city called Cape Town.

## THE SLAVE TRADE

Gold was the principal lure for the Europeans at first, but in time something more profitable was discovered, a commodity that became known as "black gold"—slaves. The slave trade was to become the most important business between Europe and Africa. Labor was required for the farms of Spain and Portugal, as well as for the plantations of São Tomé. An even bigger market for slaves was the Spanish and Portuguese colonies just beginning in the West Indies and Brazil, and later in North America. Unable to find a sufficient work force for their plantations and mines among the native peoples, the European settlers needed all the laborers they could get.

Slavery was nothing new. It had existed in many parts of the world for centuries. The Bible reports that the Egyptians had made slaves of the Hebrews, and both the Roman and Greek empires had depended on slave labor. In Africa, slavery already had a long history. Warriors captured in tribal battles might become the property of the victors, and people who broke tribal laws were sometimes punished by being sold as slaves. However, the slavery imposed on captives and criminals in Africa was different from what developed in the Americas. On New World plantations, slaves were simply property, like cattle, but in Africa slaves were more like servants. As a modern historian of Africa has written,

> Household slaves lived with their masters, often as members of the family. They could work themselves free of their obligations. They could marry their masters' daughters. They could become traders, leading men in peace and war, governors, and sometimes even kings. "A slave who knows how to serve," ran an old Ashanti proverb, "succeeds to his master's property."

When they realized the value of these slaves to the outsiders, African chiefs were willing to exchange them for European products, especially guns. During the nearly four centuries of the slave trade, an estimated 30 to 60 million human beings were transported to Europe or the Americas to be sold in slave markets. Many—some say more than half—died before they arrived.

As the demand grew and the profit increased, the business spread beyond the Portuguese. Independent slavers from many countries dealt in the valuable merchandise, and the Dutch and the English went into the business on a national scale, with government companies sponsoring wholesale trade. The temptation was very great for the Africans, who were paid handsomely to hunt and trap each other for sale to their eager buyers. Wars broke out between tribes—not, as in the past, over land disputes, but for profit.

The results of this horrible business were tragic, not only for the poor victims who were sold, but also for the societies from which they came. Trade ended between North Africa and the south because there was more profit to be had trading in human flesh with the Europeans. Many farms were abandoned, and famine spread throughout the continent, greatly reducing the population. Because the strongest and most intelligent young people fetched the highest prices, the continent lost its best potential leaders. As the fierce battles between tribes raged, villages were destroyed. But perhaps the worst consequence of the slave trade for Africa was the effect it had on the social order. Stable, peaceful societies that had grown over the centuries were shattered on both coasts of Africa.

In some ways, the effects of slavery were tragic for the slave-owners as well. Many people trace the roots of racism to that institution. Centuries of viewing Africans as subject people, fit only for physical labor, gave people a distorted view of the African as "a child of nature," a primitive, helpless creature only slightly different from a beast. Worse yet, the excuses used by slavers became a part of European and American thought. By justifying the exploitation as a benefit to the Africans, bringing them the "blessings" of Christianity and civilization, the slave trade planted a seed in the Western mind that grew into the poisonous plant of modern colonialism.

Although it was very profitable and the governments of many countries supported and even invested in it, slavery was not universally accepted. There were people in Europe and America who felt it was morally wrong and opposed it strongly. Antislavery movements sprang up and pressed for abolition. Several other factors contributed to ending the slave trade. One was that slavery began to be less profitable. The huge sugar plantations in the New World flooded the European market, and prices fell. With the introduction of new machinery, the need for physical labor dropped. And the slaves themselves grew increasingly angry about their situation. Africans had always resisted slavery as well as they could, and when slaves were settled in large numbers in North America and the Caribbean, rebellions were common. In Brazil, as early as the 17th century, a large group of slaves broke free and organized an independent black republic that lasted for over a century. Africans in Jamaica frequently escaped to the mountains and could not be recaptured. And in Haiti, which held some 400,000 slaves, a revolution in 1791 overthrew the white masters permanently.

Britain led the way in putting an end to slavery. It passed a law against it at home in 1772 and abolished slavery in its colonies in 1834. France followed suit in 1848 and ended slavery in its colonies in 1860. The United States made importation of slaves illegal in 1808, though it was not until 1865 that it emancipated the slaves already in the country.

## EUROPEAN EXPLORATION OF AFRICA

As the trade in human beings began to diminish toward the end of the 18th century, outside interest in Africa began to grow for other reasons. Still a mystery to most of the world, the interior was thought to be infinitely rich, and Europe saw commercial possibilities in opening it to trade and development. Explorers, motivated more by a spirit of adventure and scientific curiosity than by a desire for wealth, were beginning to track its rivers and discover its vast lakes. The Europeans were especially interested because they knew that these mighty waterways could serve as trade routes into the interior and could open up the heart of the continent to their own commercial development.

Such explorers as the Scottish medical missionary David Livingstone explained their reasons for visiting and mapping the continent as a desire to bring "the three Cs—Commerce, Christianity, and Civilization." Livingstone reasoned that only by introducing the European way of life to Africa could the evils of the slave trade and the misery of the native peoples be ended. He was later joined in his explorations by the American newspaperman Henry Morton Stanley, who felt the same way about the native population of the continent. Stanley described his adventures in a book called *Through the Dark Continent* (1878), a title that still offends Africans.

The spirit of the early explorers was usually sincere, if unintentionally insulting. Some Europeans wanted to share the benefits of their culture with the "less privileged" Africans. And if there was a profit to be made out of it, so much the better. The discoveries of Livingstone, Stanley, and others excited great interest in Europe. They revealed the vast wealth to be found in Africa and showed that even the most remote parts could be reached. Dr. Livingstone proved that with quinine it was possible to survive malaria, a disease that had killed many earlier visitors to the continent. The development of the steamboat made navigation of Africa's vast rivers possible. Africa began to appear a very promising frontier for exploitation.

## THE SCRAMBLE FOR AFRICA

The king of Belgium was quick to notice the possibilities. One of the wealthiest monarchs in Europe, Léopold II was very eager to increase his property still further. He had followed Stanley's career carefully and had also read other accounts of "the unspeakable riches" of the Congo. In 1876 he invited a group of explorers and geographers to his capital in Brussels and outlined a plan to "develop" the area. His official goal was "to bring light to the dark continent." As he explained at his meeting, "To open to civilization the only part of our globe where it has yet to penetrate, to pierce the darkness which envelops whole populations . . . is, I dare to say, a crusade worthy of this century of progress."

The king offered to invest his own money, made by speculating in the European stock market, in the project, and many people applauded this humanitarian gesture. But his real motives were no secret to those who knew him. He made them clear in a letter to his ambassador to England later that year, when he wrote frankly, "I do not want to miss a good chance of getting us a slice of this magnificent African cake."

Léopold created the African International Association, supposedly to set up a series of scientific stations and trading posts in the center of the continent. His purpose, he explained, was to combat slavery, to spread Christianity and civilization, and to promote free trade. In reality, he wanted to gain complete control of the Congo basin. He hired Stanley, who knew the area and the people well, to construct roads and negotiate treaties with local chiefs. Unfamiliar with European law, these African leaders could easily be persuaded to turn their land over to Léopold for very little. According to historian Robin McKown,

> One chief put his "X" on a treaty in return for a piece of cloth each month. To another, who held out a little longer, Stanley granted a red coat with gold facing, 20 red handkerchiefs, 40 red cotton caps, and 128 bottles of Dutch gin. Since none of them could read, it is obvious they had no idea what they were signing away.

What they were signing away was their countries. In a bold and shrewd business move, Léopold established the Congo Free State, so-called because the European powers that invested in it agreed to a policy of free trade, without taxes, among themselves. It was a private business venture that gave him complete control over a territory more than 77 times the size of his own country.

IN THE RUBBER COILS.

Scene—*The Congo "Free" State.*

*King Léopold of Belgium brings "Christianity and Civilization" to the Congo: cartoon by Linley Sambourne in the British humor magazine* Punch, 1903. (Courtesy General Research Division, The New York Public Library, Astor, Lenox and Tilden Foundation)

The profits of Léopold's enterprise were so great that other European countries began to think of slicing pieces of "this magnificent African cake" for themselves. Half a dozen nations began to grab territory, by diplomatic treaty if possible or by military invasion if necessary. The period came to be known as "the scramble for Africa."

European nations already had a foothold on the continent with settlements here and there, but these scattered holdings were only crumbs of the cake that they were to divide among themselves during the next 20 years. The Belgian king's success made everyone's mouth water for more. As Raymond Oliver and J. D. Fage have written, "Probably it was Léopold, more than any other single statesman, who created the 'atmosphere' of scramble."

## THE BERLIN CONFERENCE OF 1884–85

So great was the competition and so complicated the claims among European powers for land in Africa that a conference was called in Berlin in 1884 to decide who had rights to what. With lordly assurance, 13 European countries and the United States divided up the continent into "spheres of influence," assigning territory to seven of the participants and agreeing to certain policies for their mutual protection.

The arguments were fierce, but eventually everyone signed an agreement, called the Berlin Act, in 1885. In it they confirmed Léopold's right to the Congo region but determined that the Congo and Niger rivers must remain open to international commerce. The agreement established that a country had to have people actually in possession of territory before it could claim the land and that no one could take over any new land without notifying the others. In order to maintain the public appearance of acting for the benefit of the continent they were gobbling up among themselves, the act included the promise to "watch over the preservation of the native tribes, and to care for the improvement of the condition of their moral and material well-being, and to help in suppressing slavery, and especially the slave trade."

This conference didn't create the scramble, as some people have argued, but it made it official and seemed to make it legitimate. It also made it orderly. The European countries were to decide who got what by diplomatic negotiation instead of by wars among themselves, drawing lines on maps in government offices in Europe rather than on battlefields in Africa. During the 20 years that followed, France,

# CONDITIONS IN THE CONGO FREE STATE

From our country each village had to take 20 loads of rubber. . . . We had to take these loads in four times a month. . . . We got no pay. We got nothing. . . . Our village got cloth and a little salt, but not the people who did the work. . . . It used to take 10 days to get the 20 baskets of rubber—we were always in the forest to find the rubber vines, to go without food, and our women had to give up cultivating the fields and gardens. Then we starved. Wild beasts—the leopards—killed some of us while we were working away in the forest and others got lost or died from exposure or starvation and we begged the white men to leave us alone, saying we could get no more rubber, but the white men and their soldiers said: Go. You are only beasts yourselves. You are only Nyama [meat]. We tried, always going further into the forest, and when we failed and our rubber was short, the soldiers came to our towns and killed us. Many were shot, some had their ears cut off; others were tied up with ropes around their necks and bodies and taken away. . . .

We used to hunt elephants long ago and there were plenty in our forests, and we got much meat; but Bula Matari [the Congo state] killed the elephant hunters because they could not get rubber, and so we starved. We are sent out to get rubber, and when we come back with little rubber we are shot. . . . [S]ometimes we brought rubber into the white man's stations. . . . when it was not enough the white man would put some of us in lines, one behind the other, and would shoot us through all our bodies.

—Interview with Congolese villagers, 1893, from the report on conditions in the Congo Free State by British consul Roger Casement

England, Portugal, Belgium, Spain, Italy, and Germany took over almost the whole continent, partitioning it into colonies and sending their own officials to govern them.

These holdings weren't always profitable. Sometimes, in fact, they were maintained at great expense. The partition led to bitter rivalries among the colonizing nations, and sometimes to conflicts that required costly armies. Colonization also led to deep resentment among the peoples of Africa. But once it got started, the process couldn't be stopped. Even countries that didn't really want to establish new colonies in Africa felt compelled to protect the interests they already had. Great Britain, which still had unhappy memories of losing its colonies in the New World a hundred years before, was afraid that if France and Germany grew too powerful in Africa, they would interfere with its trade.

There were several other reasons why Europe entered this period of empire-building. The Industrial Revolution had begun, and the booming industries needed raw materials. Africa was a prime source of minerals, metals, rubber, palm oil (used for machine lubrication), cotton, and coal, as well as gold and diamonds. It also provided such luxuries as coffee, tea, and spices for the newly prosperous industrial countries. And as production increased, manufacturers had to look for new markets.

Greed for money was not the only motive for colonization. In justice to the Europeans, it must be admitted that some were prompted by genuine humanitarian reasons. The slave trade still existed in Africa, and many people were willing to fight, if necessary, to stamp the evil out. Missionaries were deeply involved in the beginnings of colonialism, eager to bring Christianity to the continent. The French described what they were doing in Africa as a "civilizing mission." The English saw the native people of Africa as "the white man's burden" and felt a moral responsibility to bring them the benefits of their own "superior" society.

But probably the principal force behind colonization was nationalism. There was strategic value in having control in different parts of the world, and the more land a country controlled, the more prestige it had. National pride drove people to increase their countries' holdings. Italy and Germany were still weak, disunited nations at the end of the 19th century and felt that by building empires they could become stronger. Small countries like Belgium and Portugal wanted to be able to compete with their larger neighbors.

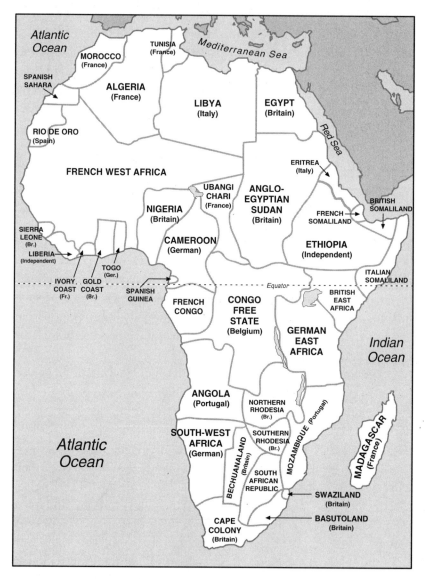

*This map shows major areas of European control in Africa around the turn-of-the-century.*

When Léopold II initiated the scramble for Africa in 1876, less than one-tenth of Africa was under foreign control. By 1903, almost all of it was. During those 27 years, Africa's map changed more than it had in the 5,000 years before. Half a century was to pass before the continent was restored to its own people and a new map could be drawn.

## CHAPTER TWO NOTES

p. 8    "Kenya would be a paradise . . ." Jomo Kenyatta, quoted in Dennis Wepman. *Jomo Kenyatta* (New York: Chelsea House, 1986), p. 53.

p. 10   "Household slaves lived with their masters. . . " Basil Davidson. *Africa in History* (New York: Collier Books, 1974), p. 182.

p. 13   "To open to civilization the only part. . . " Quoted in Thomas Pakenham. *The Scramble for Africa: 1876–1912* (New York: Random House, 1991) p. 21.

p. 13   "One chief put his 'X' on a treaty. . . " Robin McKown. *The Colonial Conquest of Africa* (New York: Franklin Watts, 1971), p. 29.

p. 15   "Probably it was Léopold. . . " Raymond Oliver and J. D. Fage. *A Short History of Africa* (London: Penguin Books, 1988), p. 61.

p. 15   ". . . watch over the preservation of the native tribes. . . " Berlin Act, 1885, Article VI, quoted Robin Hallett. *Africa Since 1875* (Ann Arbor, Mich.: University of Michigan Press, 1974), p. 433.

p. 16   "From our country . . ." Quoted in Thomas Pakenham. *The Scramble for Africa* (New York: Random House, 1991), pp. 598–99.

# THE CONTINENT
# DIVIDED

From Muhammad Muntaga, son of . . . the great sheik
Umar . . . who fought a holy war in God's name, according
to the laws of God and nothing more. . . . To . . . Colonel
Desbordes, may God confound and bring ruin on your
friends. . . . No one is more of a malefactor, no one more of
a traitor, no one more wicked than you.

You say that you only wish to open up a road for trade.
This is false and contrary to sense and reason. Your desire
is to destroy the country, to close the trade routes and make
war on Believers. . . .

The day when we meet, the birds of the air will not need
to look elsewhere for their food.

> —Letter from the governor of Nioro (in present-
> day Mali) to Colonel Gustave Borgnis-Desbordes,
> commander of the French forces, 1883

The partition of Africa was not quite as smooth and
peaceful in the field as it was in the government offices of Berlin,
London, Paris, and Lisbon, where it started, but it nevertheless took
place with surprising efficiency. In all, it took less than 20 years to divide

up the continent. The boundary lines were drawn by people who had never visited Africa. They cut through tribal lands or lumped different groups together without regard for the cultural and linguistic divisions of the native peoples. Where possible, the boundaries followed natural barriers, creating neat new parcels that had nothing to do with the historic territories of the continent.

It wasn't all done at the conference table in Berlin. European countries assumed control of African lands at different times, and in different ways. The first and easiest way was by treaty. The Europeans had been entering into trade agreements with the Africans for years, and it was not difficult to persuade the local chieftains to take the next step and enter into political ones as well. Some of these treaties included promises of economic development. More often what the Europeans offered was protection from other Europeans.

## MILITARY CONQUEST

The so-called paper partition was mostly conducted among the Europeans themselves, and it proceeded with little conflict during the first few years of negotiations. But the actual slicing of the African cake was not always so friendly. Many chieftains who had been willing to sign contracts in the palm-oil and ivory trade were not so ready to sign away the independence of their countries, and eventually the takeover of Africa became more a military than a diplomatic affair. Although the colonization of Africa was defended as bringing the three Cs—Christianity, Commerce, and Civilization—it was carried out most often by a fourth: Conquest. Many historians now prefer to speak of the "conquest," rather than the "partition," of the continent and say that it was accomplished by the three Ms: Missionaries, Merchants, and Mercenaries.

It was all done according to law, but it was the Europeans' law, the law of the Berlin Act, not the Africans'. African kings seldom gave up their power willingly when they understood what they were being asked to sign, and these treaties were forced on them by arms. There were often bitterly fought battles, but in every case the Europeans won, even though they were badly outnumbered.

It is not hard to understand why. In the first place, the Africans were accustomed to small-scale tribal conflicts and were not equipped for fighting against well-trained and well-supported European armies that could always call up reinforcements from home when they needed them. Another reason for the quick success of the invading armies was that centuries of the slave trade had divided the larger African states, and no unified army ever developed among them.

But the main explanation for the Europeans' victories was their superior equipment. Although many of the more developed African nations had guns by that time, they had old-style rifles that were no match for the British Maxim-gun, developed in 1889. This was the first mobile machine-gun, and the British government was careful to prevent any from falling into the hands of the Africans. As the English poet Hilaire Belloc wrote,

> Whatever happens, we have got
> The Maxim-gun; and they have not.

By 1900, nearly every square mile of Africa was a part of some European country's "sphere of influence." Liberia, established by the United States for freed slaves in 1822 and declared independent in 1847, and Ethiopia, a Christian kingdom that had been a free nation since the 11th century, were the only completely independent countries on the continent.

Not all Africans saw the Europeans as invaders and usurpers. To some they came as allies to protect them from other, stronger African nations. The colonizers were not slow to take advantage of the rivalries among Africans. As long as native tribes warred against each other, they could not unite against the Europeans. The strategy of "divide and conquer" was very successful in keeping native resistance isolated and fragmentary.

The management of the many scattered colonies, different though it was from place to place, had certain things in common. Since one of the main goals of colonization was the exploitation of the resources of the territories, all the European nations tried to establish peaceful communities that could work the soil and the mines profitably for them. The Europeans brought equipment for large-scale plantation farming and built roads and railways. Needing skilled labor, they created schools to train the native peoples, teaching Africans to read and write in the European languages used in trade by the colonizing country. They also brought the institutions of their own countries—the religion, the social life, and, of course, the prejudices. Some sought to turn the "backward" Africans into duplicates of their own "advanced" citizens; others found it more profitable to leave African societies intact and merely take the labor force and natural resources of the continent. But all came with a belief in the superiority of European civilization and their right to force it on the Africans. And all saw the continent as a cake to be consumed among themselves.

## PORTUGAL

Of the seven countries that established colonies in Africa, Portugal had the earliest presence there. On the Atlantic coast it held Angola, the oldest colony in Africa, and on the east coast it had Mozambique, then known as Portuguese East Africa. The Portuguese had built settlements in Africa as far back as 1481, when they founded their first trading post in present-day Ghana, and gradually they assumed control over the entire southern part of the African kingdom of Congo. In time their scattered holdings in that region became the colony of Angola, but they never held official power over their territory until the Berlin Act gave them the authority to claim it in 1885. Even then they had to fight for the land. The Portuguese conquered their territories only after long and bloody warfare, and their rule was never accepted willingly.

The Portuguese treated their colonies as a part of Portugal but exploited them very harshly. Although Africans could qualify for full Portuguese citizenship if they owned property and reached a certain educational level, very few ever attained that status. Portugal was the last European nation to abolish slavery, and even after Europe had outlawed the slave trade, Portugal continued to ship slaves from Mozambique to its own colony in Brazil. When it was no longer possible to trade in slaves directly, Portuguese colonists continued to enforce labor upon the people in their African colonies. By imposing high taxes, they required them to work under conditions that were the same as slavery.

Agitation for independence was made very difficult in the Portuguese colonies by tight police control, censorship, and close supervision of the schools. These colonies seemed permanent. As a modern historian has written, "A policy of calculated repression which discouraged literacy, withheld education, and isolated the African from the fast-changing world around him seemed ideally designed to maintain Portugal's colonial position indefinitely." But despite the rigid enforcement of these harsh laws, the Portuguese never broke the spirit of independence in the native peoples they governed. Rebellions were frequent, and although they were ruthlessly suppressed they continued to break out through Portugal's long history of colonization in Africa.

## SPAIN

The colony of Río Muñi, a tiny piece of land between Gabon and Cameroon, had been a Spanish slave-trading post since 1778. With some small islands off its coast, Río Muñi became Equatorial Guinea (sometimes called Spanish Guinea) in 1875 and was formally given to Spain as a colony by the French in 1900. A much larger, but hardly more valuable, piece of property came to Spain in 1889 when the Spanish laid claim to a tract of desert called Spanish Sahara (now Western Sahara). A small strip of northern Morocco along the Mediterranean coast completed Spain's share, the smallest and poorest European claim on the continent. There was little competition among the Europeans for Spain's holdings and a great deal of resistance within them.

The Spanish had established a financial arrangement with certain tribes in Río Muñi that resulted in relatively peaceful relations with the Africans, but Spanish efforts at compelling local people to work on their cocoa plantations provoked uprisings. Without the military resources to force the issue, the Spanish recruited their labor from Liberia and Nigeria.

## GREAT BRITAIN

The British had administered Cape Colony, in what is now South Africa, since they took it from the Dutch in 1806, and they annexed the area officially in 1814. They expanded their holdings in southern Africa and made the Union of South Africa a part of their Commonwealth in 1910. Over the years, Great Britain took control of other territories in every part of Africa. Although Britain was the least enthusiastic participant in the scramble for Africa at first, by 1914 it had assumed control of a major portion of the continent.

*Traditional silos of the Basuto tribe in the British colony of Lesotho.* (Courtesy SATOUR)

Great Britain was the only one of the colonizing nations that intended eventually to restore its colonies to independence—not for moral reasons (although many British did think it was wrong to take another people's land), but because they did not consider it very profitable. The nation's experience in America and in Asia had taught that colonization could be an expensive and uncertain business. But the British assumed it would not be for a long time.

British settlers in West Africa, who constituted a much smaller white minority than those in the east, allowed a good deal of native control, permitting the Africans to manage their own affairs and leaving tribal chiefs with much of their authority. Local laws regarding property, marriage, and inheritance were respected, and the government tried to avoid disturbing native life. Africans who met certain requirements could vote and run for office in the colonial legislature. In these colonies, the British really lived up to their promise to "prepare the African for independence."

But in Rhodesia and the eastern colonies, where there were large British settlements, British authority was exercised much more severely. Great Britain controlled the government and the courts completely. Native people had few rights and were required to work for very low wages on British farms. In Kenya, they were charged high taxes and every male over 15 was made to wear a fingerprinted I.D. card around his neck at all times, under penalty of imprisonment. Far from thinking of their African colonies as temporary, the British in Rhodesia saw them as a stepping stone to an even greater empire. Cecil Rhodes, for whom the colony was named, left his vast fortunes to a society whose goal was "the extension of British rule throughout the world . . . especially the occupation of the whole continent of Africa . . . the whole of South America. . . . The ultimate recovery of the United States as an integral part of the British Empire. . . ."

## FRANCE

The French began to stake claims to African lands in the early 19th century. In 1830 France took control of Algeria, a large Arab-held country along the northern border of the continent, and during the rest of the 19th century it extended its possessions east into Tunisia and south into and beyond the Sahara. By the time the conquest of Africa was complete, France owned most of the northwest quarter of the continent. Although the British had the richest and most widely scattered colonial holdings in Africa, France held the largest share.

Unlike the British, who maintained a strict separation between the African and the European populations in their colonies, the French had a policy called "assimilation," offering full citizenship to the people whose lands they governed. They called their colonies "overseas territories" and gave seats to African representatives in the French parliament. But while the goal of the French was equality, it was equality on French terms. As one historian has written, "It was characteristic of French rule that laws were made in Paris . . . ; the overseas governments made the detailed regulations for bringing them into force." Believing their society to be superior to that of the Africans, the French established their own laws and customs everywhere, disregarding native traditions. When the gift of their civilization was declined, they imposed it, often with brutal force.

## GERMANY

Shortly before the Berlin Conference, Germany began to look hungrily toward Africa. In 1883, its chancellor, Otto von Bismarck, took control of a small settlement on the west coast and quickly began expanding it. The native peoples of the Namib and Kalahari deserts fought desperately for their poor, barren land, but they were no match for German firearms and were forced to submit to the harsh occupation of what became German South-West Africa (now Namibia). In 1884, the Germans established a claim further north on the coast, shrewdly negotiating with chieftains for Togoland (now Togo), between present-day Ghana and Benin. The next year they secured the Cameroons (now Cameroon), between Niger and Gabon, in the same way. Wanting to establish a foothold in eastern and central Africa as well, Germany went on to acquire Tanganyika and the island of Zanzibar (now unified as Tanzania) on the east coast, and in 1895 added the small territories of Ruanda and Urundi (now Rwanda and Burundi), next to the Congo Free State.

Although the subjects of the German empire fought bitterly for freedom throughout the period of their occupation, they were never to organize an independence movement like those that finally liberated the other colonies in Africa. The German empire in Africa didn't last long enough.

When World War I ended in 1918, the League of Nations took over Germany's colonies and in 1919 distributed them to the allies who had won the war. Togoland and the Cameroons were transferred to France and England, a part of each colony given to each country. France kept its shares of the two colonies intact and separate, but England added its portion of the Cameroons to Nigeria and its part of Togoland to the Gold Coast (now Ghana). England also received Tanganyika, one of the most profitable colonies in Africa, and Zanzibar. Belgium was permitted to annex Ruanda and Urundi to its Congo colony, and the Union of South Africa, by then an independent nation governed by a white minority, was given authority to administer South-West Africa, which adjoins it. Germany's part in the colonial history of Africa lasted only a little over 30 years.

## BELGIUM

The country that started the scramble for Africa ended up with only one colony, but that one was perhaps the richest of all. The Congo Free State (now Zaire) was a private business owned by King Léopold II, whose possession of this large central African holding was made official by the Berlin Act in 1885. Rich in diamonds, gold, copper, rubber, and minerals, it was a source of enormous wealth to Léopold.

Léopold's business in Africa was conducted with unparalleled brutality. If a village failed to meet its quota of rubber or ivory, armed soldiers had orders to punish it, if necessary, by burning the village and killing its residents, as an example to others. Rape and looting were widespread and officially sanctioned. Mutilation was a common practice, as punishment and even as a way of counting the population, and soldiers were rewarded for the number of amputated right hands they collected. Murder was so common that the harvesting of rubber fell off because of lack of manpower. As many as 8 million Congolese are said to have died at the hands of Léopold's soldiers during the 23 years he ran his profitable business in Africa. In time the atrocities committed there became such a scandal in Europe that a commission was called in Brussels to investigate them. In 1908, the king was forced to sell his property to the Belgian government, which declared it a colony, renamed it the Belgian Congo, and greatly reformed its management.

The policies of the new colony were in most ways more humane than they had been. Conscious that the other countries participating in the Berlin Act were waiting hopefully to claim pieces of the rich territory if Belgium was stripped of it, the government in Brussels instituted modern medical facilities, provided education, housing, and insurance, and paid reasonable wages for the work they exacted. They called their system "paternalism," acting like fathers to the Africans—and expecting the obedience of children in return. They never officially established a racial barrier to professional advancement, but they did not believe in giving the Africans any say in their own government, either, and did nothing to prepare them for independence. No political rights were allowed, and only the most elementary education was provided. The schooling available to the Congolese was limited to instruction in basic literacy, religion, and trade skills, to keep anyone from getting any dangerous ideas. But people got them anyway. Despite the "paternal" treatment of the Belgians, the Congolese were among the first to seek independence.

## ITALY

The Italians received nothing from the League of Nations when the former German empire was doled out to the other countries that had defeated Germany, and it hadn't had much of a foothold in Africa before. The last of the European powers to join the competition for land on the continent, Italy managed to stake a small claim by negotiation or by armed conquest. It acquired a piece of Somaliland (now Somalia), on the Indian Ocean, in 1889, the Ethiopian province of Eritrea, on the Red Sea, in 1890, and the large but barren nation of Libya, then the poorest in Africa, on the Mediterranean coast, in 1911. None of these territories was particularly valuable at that time, but they had strategic importance, and Italy always had ambitions for a larger slice of the African cake.

In 1896, Italy invaded Ethiopia from Eritrea but was routed in what has been called "the bloodiest defeat ever endured by a colonial power in Africa." Nearly 40 years later, in 1935, Italy tried again, from its own country. This time it was fully equipped with modern armaments, poison gas, and air power, while the Ethiopians had only ancient rifles and swords with which to defend themselves. Italy's bombing of the Ethiopian city of Dessie, destroying hospitals and schools as well as military targets, was the first air raid in history, and it so shattered its victim's defenses that the African nation surrendered a few months later. More a military occupation than a colonization, the Italians' control of Ethiopia lasted until 1941, when the British helped organize a guerrilla force that ousted them.

The entire period of African colonization lasted less than a century, but it changed the course of the continent's history more than the 5,000 years of civilization that preceded it. If European occupation destroyed many of Africa's ancient cultures and undermined its social order, it also introduced the Industrial Revolution and brought the continent into contact with the rest of the world. Europeans built railroads that linked remote areas of the continent, and taught the Africans how to run them. And with the bringing of education—reluctantly provided but necessary for the operation of its many enterprises—colonialism planted the seeds of its own destruction.

With the introduction of Western education, Africans came to know their place in the larger world picture, and to rediscover the pride and dignity that the harsh laws of European colonization had suppressed. A new African elite emerged, and with it, inevitably, a vision of political independence. In time, that vision was to sweep the continent.

# ETHIOPIA

The oldest independent country in Africa, Ethiopia has been conquered but has never been colonized in its 3,000-year history. According to tradition, Ethiopia was created by King Solomon of Israel for the Queen of Sheba after the birth of their son Menelik I in the 10th century B.C.

There are many legends about the early days of the region, but historians agree that about 200 B.C. the descendants of the first people living there created a kingdom around the town of Axum, which is still standing in northern Ethiopia. Merchants from Egypt, Greece, and India traded in gold, silver, copper, skins, ivory, spices, and glassware there. The Axumite kingdom, whose rulers traveled in elephant-drawn chariots and had tame giraffes in their palace gardens, was one of the wonders of the ancient world. Early in the fourth century its kings were converted to Christianity, and Axum became the first Christian kingdom in Africa. When trade declined in the 10th century A.D., the kingdom became weak, and for several hundred years each of the country's different regions had its own ruler, but in 1260 the rule of the descendants of the Queen of Sheba was restored to a unified Ethiopia.

Europe had long looked hungrily at this rich empire, with its strategic location on the Red Sea as an important African point of entry from India and Arabia. In 1869 Italy began a series of invasions, and by 1885 it occupied some territory in the kingdom. Europe supported Italy's efforts at increasing its holdings in Ethiopia, but in 1896 the troops of Emperor Menelik II won a crushing victory at Adowa, the first time an African nation defeated a European army in a major battle, and Italy was forced to retreat. Although the Italians still occupied the province of Eritrea, Ethiopia's triumph in Adowa was an inspiration for other African nations to organize against European rule in the 20th century.

In 1930, a son of one of Menelik's cousins, Ras (Prince) Tafari Makonnen, became emperor with the title Haile Selassie, which means "Power of the Trinity." When Italy

*Haile Selassie, emperor of Ethiopia (1903–74). (Courtesy United Nations YN/mh)*

invaded again in 1935 and conquered the capital, Addis Ababa, the next year, the new emperor went into exile. Italy combined Ethiopia and a portion of Somalia, renaming the area Italian East Africa. Haile Selassie made a moving plea for justice to the League of Nations in 1937, stating, "I declare in the face of the whole world that the emperor, the government, and the people of Ethiopia will not bow before force." Newspapers all over the world praised the emperor as the conscience of humanity, but the League did nothing to help his country. When some Ethiopians tried to assassinate the Italian military commander that year, 30,000 Ethiopians were executed as a punishment.

When World War II broke out, Britain came to Ethiopia's aid, and together they drove the Italians from the country in 1941. Four years later, Ethiopia became one of the charter members of the United Nations, and Haile Selassie was a guiding force in the establishment of the Organization of African Unity in his capital. Because it remains the OAU's headquarters, Addis Ababa has been called "the Capital of Africa."

After 44 years as emperor, Haile Selassie was overthrown in 1974 and died a few months later. A military government took control of Ethiopia and instituted a socialist government like that of the Soviet Union, distributing the land more equally and establishing economic, social, and educational reforms. The victim of tragic famines in 1981 and 1988, the country has suffered deep problems, but it has progressed steadily and remains a focal point for African independence and unity.

# NÉGRITUDE

The sense of racial identity that grew up among both Africans and African-Americans in the early part of the 20th century was the consciousness of a cultural heritage that unified them and set them apart. This ethnic spirit is deeper than a historical relationship. It is a bond linking black people wherever they are, including those in Africa and the Americas. It is not a political idea, but rather a spiritual and psychological one involving a set of shared values. The term for this sense of a common black heritage, coined in the African-French community of Martinique in the West Indies, is *Négritude*.

First used in print by the Martiniquan poet Aimé Césaire in 1938, the word *Négritude* defined a revolutionary spirit that recognized and protested against racism of all sorts, not only political, but also economic and social. In the long poem that first expressed the idea publicly, *Notes on a Return to the Native Land*, Césaire rejects modern "white" civilization and celebrates the natural African landscape, calling for black people to value the unique spirit of their own race. The poem is considered a political statement because it attacks colonialism, but it is also a psychological work because it examines the effect of colonialism on the mind. Césaire's poem became the bible of Négritude, expressing the warm, generous, emotional character of the black in contrast to the cold, commercial, spirit of Western civilization.

## CHAPTER THREE NOTES

p. 20    "From Muhammad Muntago . . ." Letter from the governor of Nioro (in present-day Mali) to Colonel Gustave Borgnis-Desbordes, commander, French forces, 1883, quoted in Thomas Pakenham. *The Scramble for Africa* (New York: Random House, 1991), pp. 171–72.

p. 24    "A policy of calculated repression. . ." Robert July. *A History of the African People* (New York: Charles Scribner's Sons, 1970), p. 485.

The positive feeling about blackness that defines Négritude found a warm response among black intellectuals in the United States, the West Indies, Europe, and Africa itself. One of the most celebrated poets of that continent, Léopold Senghor, a friend of Césaire and later the first president of Senegal, became a major contributor to the poetry of Négritude. For Senghor, Négritude is something more personal, an expression of the spiritual depth, wholeness, and vitality of Africans, as expressed in their approach to life, work, and art. In his poem "New York," Senghor invites the cold American city to draw vitality and strength from Africa and the Africans:

> New York, I say to you: New York let black blood
> flow into your blood
> That it may rub the rust from your steel joints,
> like an oil of life. . . .
> Now return the most ancient times, the unity recovered. . . .
> Thought linked to act, ear to heart, sign to sense. . . .

The Négritude movement was most successful and reached its highest expression in France, the French West Indies, and French-speaking West Africa, but it had an influence on art and thought worldwide, and, indirectly, on the political destiny of the continent that gave birth to it. Not itself a political philosophy, Négritude gave poetic form to the spirit of racial pride that inspired and nourished the demand for national independence.

p. 26    "The extension of British rule throughout the world . . ." John Gilbert Lockhart and Christopher Montague Woodhouse. *Cecil Rhodes* (New York: Macmillan, 1963), pp. 69–70.

p. 26    "It was characteristic of French rule. . . " Lucy Mair. *The New Africa* (London: C. A. Watts, 1967), p. 35.

p. 33    "New York I say to you: . . ." Léopold Senghor, translated by Arnold von Bradshaw, in Gerald Moore and Ulla Beier, eds. *Modern Poetry from Africa* (Baltimore: Penguin, 1966), p. 237.

# FOREIGN SUPPORT FOR AFRICAN INDEPENDENCE

The colored peoples will not always submit to foreign domination. . . . These nations and races, composing as they do the vast majority of humanity, are going to endure this treatment just as long as they must and not a moment longer. Then they are going to fight, and the War of the Color Line will outdo in savage inhumanity any war this world has yet seen. For colored folk have much to remember and they will not forget.

—W. E. B. Du Bois in his "The African Roots of War" (1914)

Although the people of Africa were politically isolated, national independence movements there received some encouragement from outside the continent. The idea of freedom for Africa inspired much sympathy in Europe and the New World. As far back as the 18th century, organizations opposed to slavery and imperialism were at work in England to make it possible for blacks to go back to their home continent. In 1787, a settlement was established in Sierra Leone, on the west coast of Africa, as a free city for that purpose. In the United States, the Free African Society of Newport, Rhode Island, proposed "the return of Africans to Africa" in 1791, and with the establishment 31 years later of Liberia, next to Sierra Leone, the nation made a start in realizing that dream.

## THE REPATRIATION MOVEMENT

Several other movements existed in the United States to "re-patriate" Africans by enabling them to return and create independent states in their original homeland before the beginning of the Civil War in 1861, but it wasn't until the emancipation of the slaves that the idea began to gain momentum. Probably the leading African-American voice for the building of a free nation in Africa was the West Indian writer Edward Wilmot Blyden, who had moved to Liberia in 1850 and returned to North America to promote it as a homeland for blacks during the Civil War. His eloquent book, *Liberia's Offering: The Call of Providence to the Descendants of Africa*, published in New York in 1862, was the most influential text on black nationalism of its time, and the principles of racial pride it contains anticipate many ideas of later African leaders.

A more practical application of Blyden's philosophy came in various organized efforts at what he called "re-emigration." One of the most important of these projects, although ultimately unsuccessful, was the one begun by Martin R. Delany, a free African-American from the U.S. South.

Delany, a Harvard-educated physician, organized the National Emigration Convention of Colored Men in 1854 in Cleveland, Ohio, to promote black settlement outside the United States. Originally thinking of South or Central America as more practical, he later visited Liberia, where he was warmly welcomed by Blyden, and went on to Nigeria, where he signed an agreement with the local chiefs to settle African-Americans there. As he wrote in 1861,

Africa is our fatherland and we are its legitimate descendants. . . .
I have determined to leave to my children the inheritance of a

country, the blessings of a national education and the indisputable rights of self government. . . . Our policy must be . . . Africa for the African race and black men to rule them.

Delany's re-emigration plan did not work out. The African chiefs repudiated the agreement, and the outbreak of the American Civil War turned people's minds toward matters closer to home. Delany himself gave it up, joined the Union army as the first African-American army surgeon in the United States, and went on to become a distinguished scholar. But his ringing words written in support of a black national homeland have proved prophetic. They have inspired African-Americans and Africans alike.

During the last half of the 19th century, as more and more of the territory of Africa was settled by Europeans, other organizations for the resettlement of freed slaves formed, in both the United States and England, but none of them ever came to anything. It was not until a new century dawned that the seeds planted by such pioneers as Blyden and Delany were to take root and grow.

## BLACK DISSATISFACTION

The conditions of blacks in both the New World and Africa were at a low ebb at the turn of the century. The slaves freed after the Civil War in the United States were frustrated by social conditions as bad as slavery had been. Racial segregation was instituted throughout the South. African-Americans were denied the vote and had little opportunity for jobs. Lynchings increased from about 100 a year in the 1870s to 235 in 1898, and in that year there were violent race riots in several cities. In the West Indies, there were natural disasters: The sugar crop failed, and severe hurricanes ruined the already fragile economy.

In Africa things were even worse. In the early days of English colonization, Africans had some hope of progressing toward equality in business and of a place in government, but by the end of the 19th century colonial laws had been passed that kept Africans from advancing beyond the level of laborers, servants, and low-level office workers. High "hut taxes" on all residences were imposed in Sierra Leone, and in Bechuanaland (now Botswana) and Rhodesia (now Zambia and Zimbabwe), conditions were so bad for the native peoples that insurrections broke out and were bloodily suppressed by the British. The beginnings of apartheid (pronounced, appropriately, "apart-hate")— the discriminatory system of separation of the races that kept the non-white population from any social or economic equality—were appearing in South Africa and South-West Africa (present-day Namibia).

## PAN-AFRICANISM

These conditions caused deep concern among intellectuals, both black and white, and several organizations were formed in Europe and the United States to protest and improve the situation. Among the first and most prominent was the African Association, organized in 1897 by a Trinidadian lawyer named Henry Sylvester Williams.

Educated in London and practicing law there, Wiliams had numerous African clients with land claims in their native countries against the new colonial governments, and he came to realize the injustice of the colonial system. The group he created, made up of black Africans and West Indians along with a few white sympathizers, sought to

encourage a feeling of unity [and] promote and protect the interests of all subjects claiming African descent, wholly or in part, in British colonies and other places, especially in Africa, by circulating accurate information on all subjects affecting their rights and privileges . . . and by direct appeals to the Imperial and local governments.

The African Association never became very large, but it was a politically active lobby and received considerable support both in Europe and in Africa. By 1898 it had grown enough to announce an international conference, which took place from July 23rd to the 25th, 1900, in London.

The Pan-African Conference, as it was called, had only 32 participants, 11 each from the United States and the British West Indies, five from England, four from Africa, and one from Canada. It took its name (meaning "All African") from such then popular terms as *Pan-American* and *Pan-Slav*, applied to groups seeking to unify the peoples of different countries. Its proclaimed objective was "to influence public opinion on . . . conditions affecting the welfare of the native in various parts of the world, viz. South Africa, West Africa, West Indies, and United States of America."

The meetings were taken seriously by the British public and treated respectfully by the government. The bishop of London addressed the group, and a reception was held for the participants at the House of Commons. But the conference did not have much direct effect. The petition its members sent to Queen Victoria for justice in South Africa and Southern Rhodesia was received with polite indifference and produced no action. The Pan-African Association (as the African Association was called from then on) quietly dissolved the following year. But its conference was to have important consequences. It put the word *Pan-African* in the dictionary, and it put an idea in the public consciousness.

## W. E. B. DU BOIS

Among the delegates to the Pan-African Conference was a 32-year-old professor of sociology from Atlanta University named William Edward Burghardt Du Bois who went on to become the leading spokesman for the Pan-African idea, carrying it not only to the United States and Europe but finally to Africa itself. The principal author of an appeal "To the Nations of the World" in the official *Report of the Pan-African Conference*, he wrote, "The problem of the 20th century is the problem of the color line." He was to become one of the most influential (and controversial) black protest leaders in the world and remained a major voice for justice until his death at the age of 95. W. E. B. Du Bois was one of the founders of the National Association for the Advancement of Colored People (NAACP) and the editor of its magazine, *Crisis*, for 25 years, and he wrote many books to promote his belief that all people of African descent should work together in their struggle for freedom. During the next four decades he organized several Pan-African congresses, in Paris, Brussels, Lisbon, New York, and elsewhere, which shaped the thinking not only of African-Americans but of future African leaders in many countries.

At Du Bois's fifth and last Pan-African congress, held in 1945 at the headquarters of the Pan-African Federation in Manchester, England, the attendance was widely international; there were delegates from Sierra Leone, Nigeria, the Gold Coast, Gambia, Liberia, Uganda, Tanganyika, Nyasaland, Kenya, and South Africa. Among the participants were Kwame Nkrumah of the Gold Coast (now Ghana), Jomo Kenyatta of Kenya, and Hastings Banda of Nyasaland (now Malawi). All were to lead their people to independence and become the first presidents of their countries.

The spirit of Pan-Africanism had by then become unmistakably anti-imperialist and even revolutionary. The congress's opposition to colonialism was emphatically stated:

*African-American educator and writer W. E. B. Du Bois, working in his office around 1950.* (Courtesy The New York Public Library, Schomburg Center for Research in Black Culture)

# W. E. B. DU BOIS
## (1868–1963)

The American sociologist and political activist William Edward Burghardt Du Bois was one of the most influential African-American intellectuals of the 20th century. In his writings, public addresses, and organizational leadership he profoundly influenced social and political thought both in the United States and in Africa.

Born in Great Barrington, Massachusetts, Du Bois studied at Fisk University, a black institution in Nashville, Tennessee (1885–88), the University of Berlin, Germany (1892–94), and Harvard University, from which he received a Ph.D. in history in 1895. His doctoral dissertation, *The Suppression of the Slave Trade to the United States of America, 1638–1870*, was published in 1896. A pioneering scholar in race relations in the United States, he did the first practical research on the conditions of African-American life, producing many articles and books while teaching at Atlanta University in Georgia from 1897 to 1914.

Du Bois combined a distinguished career in teaching and research with a very active one of protest for racial equality and liberation. In his famous 1903 book *The Souls of Black Folk*, he attacked the idea that African-Americans should patiently accept social and professional discrimination until they earned the acceptance of the white majority, urging instead an active

We are determined to be free. We want education. We want the right to earn a decent living, the right to express our thoughts . . . and emotions. We demand for Black Africa autonomy and independence. We will fight in every way we can for liberty, democracy, and social betterment. . . .

The delegates to the Pan-African Congress believe in peace. . . . Yet if the western world is still determined to rule mankind by force, Africans, as a last resort, may have to appeal to force in the effort to achieve Freedom, even if force destroys them and the world.

struggle for social and economic equality. In 1909 he helped found the National Association for the Advancement of Colored People (NAACP), whose monthly magazine *The Crisis*, he edited until 1934. In that year he resigned from the organization because he felt it was directing its attention to the middle class instead of to the masses.

Although he argued strongly for racial integration in the United States, Du Bois also worked for African nationalism. He was a leader in the Pan-African movement, which believed that all people of African descent should work together for freedom and equality, and he organized important meetings for the cause in 1900, 1919, and 1927 to promote the ideal of African independence and unity.

In the 1950s, Du Bois became involved in pro-Russian activities and was arrested as an unregistered foreign agent. he was acquitted in court, but his passport was revoked, and he came under constant government pressure. At last, disillusioned with the United States, he joined the Communist Party in 1961 and the next year renounced his American citizenship and moved to Ghana.

In his 70-year career, W. E. B. Du Bois published 19 books, edited four magazines, and wrote hundreds of articles on the folk culture of his people and on the African and African-American struggle for liberty. An eloquent spokesman for racial justice, he made an important contribution to social and political reform both at home and in the newly emerging nations of Africa.

The note of warning was clear, and whether or not the colonial powers chose to listen, there were those in Africa who heard it and were led to action.

## REVIVAL OF THE BACK-TO-AFRICA MOVEMENT

The philosophical principles of Pan-Africanism appealed to intellectuals and worked quietly in their minds to produce political ferment in colonial Africa, but a more direct and dramatic appeal to the masses came from another source. As conditions for African-Americans grew progressively worse, the back-to-Africa idea re-emerged in the United

# LIBERIA

The first self-governing black nation in Africa, Liberia was never officially a colony and thus has never required liberation. It was founded in 1822 by the American Colonization Society as a settlement for free African-Americans. During its first 50 years, some 13,000 freed slaves immigrated to the settlement, and nearly 6,000 slaves taken off ships illegally transporting them were released there. The settlement was originally called Monrovia, for U.S. president James Monroe, but as it grew the settlers named their new home "Liberia" (from the Latin *liber*, meaning "free"), keeping the name Monrovia for its capital city.

On July 26, 1847, the Americo-Liberians, as the settlers called themselves, declared themselves an independent republic, with the motto "Love of Liberty brought us here." It created a government and a constitution based closely on those of the United States, and the descendants of the American slaves who settled the land remained the ruling class.

From Liberia's beginning, conflict existed between the settlers and the local tribes from whom they acquired their land, often by force. There were also charges that the Americo-Liberians continued practicing slavery until the 1930s. However the nation maintained a relatively stable economy and government and escaped the European partition of Africa with the loss of relatively little land.

States. After the Civil War, interest in "re-emigration" and the establishment of an independent black state in Africa had died down, but it never disappeared completely, and by the beginning of the First World War it was coming back to life. In 1913 a mysterious figure calling himself "Chief Sam" appeared among the African-American farmers in Oklahoma. He claimed to be from the Gold Coast and offered to sell shares in an "African trade and emigration" company, including free passage back to their "fatherland," for about $25 apiece. Times were especially hard in Oklahoma then, and lynchings were frequent. Many

Liberia's economy was based on its exports of coffee (said to be the world's finest), cane sugar, and wood from which a dye was made. But during the first part of the 20th century, Brazil took over the world market in coffee, European beet sugar replaced cane sugar in popularity, and the Germans developed synthetic dyes. The salvation of Liberia came from the Firestone Tire and Rubber Company, a United States firm, which leased almost a million acres of rubber-tree forest in the 1920s and built modern highways to carry the crude rubber to the coast.

From 1877 to 1980, Liberia recognized only one political party, controlled by descendants of the original settlers. In 1980 Liberian president William R. Tolbert Jr. was overthrown and replaced by rebel leader Samuel K. Doe, who established a multiparty system in the country. Nine years later, one of Doe's soldiers, Charles Taylor, led a second rebellion. Doe was captured, tortured, and killed, and Taylor declared himself president. Taylor's party, the National Patriotic Reconstruction Assembly, has established a new capital in the inland city of Gbarnga, but a five-nation west African group has refused to recognize the government.

Despite its internal problems, Liberia has been an important voice in international affairs. It was one of the founders of the United Nations in 1945 and has been chosen to host several meetings of international organizations. As the oldest independent republic on the continent, Liberia was influential in the creation of the Organization of African Unity (OAU) in 1963.

desperate families were persuaded, and in 1914 some 60 hopefuls set out for Africa on the steamship Liberia.

Although Chief Sam kept his bargain, the venture was not a success. The liner was kept in the Liberian port of Freetown for nearly two months, and everyone was forced to pay an extra "tax" of about $125. By the time the emigrants reached the Gold Coast in 1915, they were already very disappointed.

The newcomers were well received by the local Africans, but they found life in their dreamed-of homeland a lot harder than they had expected. Many died of local diseases, and the group was no better able to integrate itself into society in Africa than it had been in America. After a year or so, most of the survivors went back to Oklahoma, and Alfred C. Sam disappeared from the scene.

But if the episode was a failure, it had some positive consequences for Pan-Africanism. It promoted a feeling of unity among African-Americans, reminding them of the possibility of independence, and it prepared the way for other, more effective efforts.

## MARCUS GARVEY AND THE UNIA

Most of the advocates of a return of African-Americans to Africa as a land of opportunity were basically businessmen, promoting their enterprises for profit, but one man stood out from the rest for the breadth of his vision, the magnetism of his personality, and the eloquence of his oratory. This was Marcus Aurelius Garvey, who soon became the only serious rival to W. E. B. Du Bois and his Pan-African movement.

A native of Jamaica in the British West Indies, Marcus Garvey was filled with the dream of uniting and improving the conditions of people of African descent. After traveling widely in the Caribbean, South and Central America, and England, the 24-year-old enthusiast returned to Jamaica in 1914 to launch the Universal Negro Improvement and Conservation Association and African Communities League, usually called by the shorter name the Universal Negro Improvement Association (UNIA). It had much more ambitious goals than anything Blyden, Delany, or Du Bois had ever claimed:

> to establish a Universal Confraternity among the race; to promote the spirit of black pride and love; to reclaim the fallen; to administer to and assist the needy; to assist in civilizing the backward tribes of Africa; to establish a central nation for the race; . . . to establish universities, colleges, academies, and schools for racial education and culture for the people. . . .

and much more. Originally intended for his fellow Jamaicans only, the UNIA soon sought wider horizons, and in 1918 Garvey transferred its headquarters to New York City, where it found a warm reception.

Garvey was snubbed by intellectuals like Du Bois, who considered him an extremist, but his public following soared into the millions. He opened branches in many large cities in the United States, and within a year the UNIA had offices in Chicago, Detroit, Pittsburgh, Philadelphia, and Cleveland. His newspaper, *Negro World*, reported the glories of African history and culture and argued that blacks must achieve economic independence. To achieve that goal he created the Negro Factories Corporation and built a hotel and a chain of restaurants, laundries, and grocery stores. His most ambitious venture was the Black Star Line, established both to ship freight between the United States and Africa and to transport people to their new homeland.

Garvey had a genius for showmanship and organized public events on a grand scale. His colorful parades in Harlem and his giant rallies won him tremendous popular support, but they also earned him the dislike of more moderate African-American leaders, and when he had himself elected "Provisional President of Africa" at the first UNIA Convention of Negroes in 1920 he was dismissed by many as a charlatan or a fanatic.

Garvey negotiated for land in Liberia, where he hoped to build a base of operations in Africa that would give him a foothold for his "central nation for the race." At first he was welcomed, but the Liberian government (with some pressure from the British and the French, who sensed a threat to their colonial power) reversed itself and banned the UNIA in that country. A campaign against him launched by rival African-American leaders, including Du Bois, led to a charge of illegally selling Black Star Line shares through the mail, and in 1925 Garvey was sentenced to five years in prison. U.S. president Calvin Coolidge freed him two years later but deported him to Jamaica, and the UNIA was scattered to the winds.

Garveyism, with its grandiose dreams of establishing an African empire, came to a sad end, but Garvey's appeal to racial pride contributed greatly to a consciousness of Africa among African-Americans, and his message spread to other parts of the world. Like Du Bois, he addressed the problems of all members of his race, at home and abroad, and stimulated Africans no less than African-Americans to recognize the possibility of taking control of their political and economic destinies. Kwame Nkrumah honored Garvey's influence on nationalism in

Africa by naming Ghana's fleet of ships the Black Star Line and putting a black star on his country's flag.

W. E. B. Du Bois gave a theoretical basis for much revolutionary thought in Africa, and during his long life (he died in 1963) he participated directly in bringing several new nations to birth. Garvey had more of an emotional appeal and spoke more to the common man. Kwame Nkrumah, recalling his college days, reported that the political theories of communists and socialists influenced him in his revolutionary ideas, "but of all the literature that I studied, the book that did more than any other to fire my enthusiasm was the *Philosophy and Opinions* of Marcus Garvey."

Sporadic attempts at resettling African-Americans in Africa occurred for over a century in the United States; Pan-Africanism was an active movement for some 40 years; Garvey's UNIA lasted only about five. But if these dreams of a united and free Africa had little practical effect in their own times, their ultimate effect was incalculable. Almost always failures in themselves, they set ideas in motion that toppled empires and, at last, freed a continent.

## CHAPTER FOUR NOTES

p. 34      "The colored peoples will not always submit . . ." W. E. B. Du Bois. "The African Roots of War." *Atlantic Monthly*, May 1914, p. 713.

pp. 35–36 "Africa is our fatherland . . ." Martin R. Delany. *Official Report of the Niger Valley Exploring Party.* New York, 1861, quoted in Emanuel Geiss. *The Pan-American Movement* (New York: Africana, 1974), p. 52.

p. 37      ". . . encourage a feeling of unity . . ." *Report of the Pan-African Congress held at the 23rd, 24th and 25th July, 1900, at Winchester Town Hall, Westminster S. W., London.* London, 1900, p. 1., quoted in Geiss, pp. 177–78.

pp. 37–38 ". . . to influence public opinion . . ." *Report*, p. 3, quoted in Geiss, p. 180.

p. 40      "We are determined to be free . . ." George Padmore, ed. *History of the Pan-African Congress* (London: Hammersmith, 1947), p. 5.

p. 44   "... to establish a Universal Confraternity ..." Marcus Garvey. *Philosophy and Opinions*, vol. II (New York, Atheneum, 1923–26), p. 37.

p. 46   ".... but of all the literature that I studied ..." Kwame Nkrumah. *Ghana: The Autobiography of Kwame Nkrumah* (New York, International Publishers 1957), p. 37.

# DESPERATE BEGINNINGS

Jesus, Savior for the Elect and Savior for us all.
We will be the conquerors sent by Thee.
The Kingdom is ours. We have it.
They, the Whites, have it no longer.
> —Hymn from the Kimbanguist Church's
> *Chants du Ciel* (*Songs from Heaven*)

Although the resistance that finally won independence from foreign political domination in Africa was volcanic, erupting in a few short years and spreading like molten lava, opposition to alien rule had been present from the very beginnings of European conquest. The European newspapers seldom reported the conflicts that broke out, and when they did they used a vocabulary that made these rebellions seem like something else. According to the press in England, the Europeans had "governments," "police," and "armies," that maintained "peace" and "order"; the Africans had "tribes" and "terrorists," guilty of "violence" and "revolt." The suppression of these uprisings, however brutal, was always called "pacification."

The protest against the Europeans who took their lands, property, and labor was sometimes inspired and supported by outside influences,

*Xhosa uprising against the Boer settlers in South Africa, painting by T. Baines, in the Africana Museum, Pretoria.* (Courtesy State Information Office, Pretoria)

but it also grew up spontaneously, and as often as it arose and was crushed, it was reborn. It took different forms in different times and places. In the early days of colonialism, resistance was usually local and brief, and the colonists crushed it ruthlessly to set an example. Generally it was military, but sometimes it took the form of religious movements. Most of the early uprisings were so small and weak that they went almost unnoticed by the rest of the world, but some took place on a large scale. A few, like the Ethiopians' defense of their nation against the Italians in 1896, even succeeded for a while. Though they seemed hopeless, these heroic efforts kept the dream of independence alive in the African spirit and served as an inspiration for the political movements to come.

## MILITARY MOVEMENTS

Resistance to colonialism began with the first invasions of the land, and it occurred everywhere. One legendary opponent of European domination was Samori Touré, a professional soldier who built a powerful

West African empire that resisted French conquest for years. From his first encounter, in 1882, when he defeated a French attack, Samori Touré fought brilliantly, negotiating with the British in Sierra Leone for arms and outmaneuvering the French repeatedly. When his empire was shattered, he moved east and created a new one in the Ivory Coast, again establishing a stable centralized state. But after more than 15 years the superior forces and equipment of the French finally defeated him. He was captured (at the age of 68) in 1898, after what has been described as "the longest series of campaigns against a single enemy in the history of French Sudanese conquest." Samori Touré lost his empires and failed to rout the French, but he brought daring, intelligence, and tactical brilliance to the struggle for independence and became one of the models for young African nationalists a half-century later.

The Germans generally tried to persuade native chiefs to sign over their territories. When this failed, they issued orders. But their orders were not always obeyed. A dramatic early example of such defiance was the conflict with the Yao tribe in southwest Tanganyika (now Tanzania) in 1891. After sweeping easily along the coast of Tanganyika, meeting all resistance with heavy gunfire and naval bombardment, the Germans turned toward the interior. Here the native peoples proved harder to conquer. The Germans attempted to negotiate and sent word to the most influential Yao chief, Machemba, that he was to come to the coast to meet with them. His reply has become legendary:

> I have heard your words, but I do not see any reason why I should obey you. I should rather die. . . . If it is a matter of friendship, I shall not refuse you, today and always, but I shall not be your subject. . . . If you want to fight, I am prepared, but never shall I be your subject. . . . Since I was born I have not set foot on the coast; shall I go there now because you call me? I shall not come. If you are strong enough, come and get me.

They did, in three bloody expeditions, burning every village and machine-gunning every African they encountered on the way, until Machemba surrendered.

The campaign to punish Machemba for his insolence was a minor battle in the ongoing war of German conquest in Africa. Other, far more serious ones came almost without cease in the years that followed, until at last the League of Nations accomplished what native resistance failed to do and stripped Germany of its colonies in 1919.

The Portuguese met native opposition long before the Berlin Act made their claims official. At first they tried to keep the peace by agreeing to pay tribute to the rulers of the lands they occupied, but by the 1880s they felt secure enough to stop paying. The Africans at once responded by attacking. The skirmishes continued for years, until in 1904 a full-scale war broke out in Angola—a war that lasted for 12 years. In 1914 and early 1915 the Portuguese were forced to give way, and the southern part of the colony was free of all European control for a time, but the next year a famine so weakened the Africans that the colonists were able to restore their power. Even then, it required an additional force of 11,000 soldiers sent from Portugal to do it.

Resistance to conquest was only the first stage of native rebellion in Africa; as the realities of the colonial system became clear to the subject peoples, rejection of alien rule appeared even among those who had accepted the Europeans at first.

When the British declared Sierra Leone a protectorate in 1896, they determined that the Africans would have to support its administration by paying a tax on each house. This "hut tax"—so called because almost all the houses in Sierra Leone except those of the administrators were in fact huts—was too much for a population that was hardly able to support itself under colonial rule. The new tax met with peaceful protests at first when it went into effect on January 1, 1898. A group of native chiefs sent a long, touching letter to the authorities, pleading, "We are not able to pay for our houses. Because we have no power and no strength to do so, so that please tell the Governor we beg him to be sorry for us, and to consider the old agreement he made with our fathers." When the governor ignored the letter, the mood changed, and one of the authors of the letter, a noted war chief named Kai Bureh, organized a rebellion. The "Hut Tax War" spread throughout the protectorate and lasted until Kai Bureh was captured in November. The victors dealt leniently with the rebels, deporting the aged war chief and declaring a general amnesty, but they did not cancel the tax.

The uprising was not a serious threat to British rule, but it made the colonists nervous. They rightly guessed that it was not merely a protest against a specific colonial policy. It reflected a bitterness at foreign control and a desire for freedom that were sure to reassert themselves. Like Samori Touré, Kai Bureh was a skillful warrior who showed that the foreigners could be challenged, and like him he became a hero and a legend. He is still spoken of reverently in Sierra Leone as "the Big Black General" who stood up to British rule.

No part of the continent was so continuously in rebellion throughout the period of colonization as Central Africa, occupied by the British in Nyasaland and Northern Rhodesia (now Malawi and Zambia), the Portuguese in Angola and Mozambique, and the Belgians in the Congo (now Zaire). From 1885, when occupation of the region began, until 1918, when World War I ended, there were more than 20 major insurrections, some lasting for years. At first, most of them were led by native kings who already had armies and the resources to negotiate for arms and ammunition, but in time many were organized by angry farmers, merchants, and soldiers, who mobilized the support of their countrymen. Among the most effective in stimulating anticolonial sentiment and the will to resist were religious leaders, who acted from spiritual rather than political motives.

## RELIGIOUS MOVEMENTS

Missionaries were among the first Europeans to settle in Africa, bringing what many felt was the most important of the three Cs that colonialism boasted, Christianity. Their gift to African life was perhaps the most honest and unselfish, and it was widely accepted in some areas. But one of the negative effects of the new religion was that it had no respect for native cultures, and Africans had as little chance of equality in the Europeans' church as they had in the Europeans' businesses or governments. Even the smartest and most willing converts could never hope to be more than followers in the white man's religion. Christianity taught equality, but the European missionaries were masters and Africans were their servants.

A result of this frustrating situation was the development of separate African Christian groups, called Ethiopian churches, which adapted Christianity to native customs and ideas and rejected European church control, and thus, indirectly, European political domination. Some of these groups were led by whites who recognized the contradiction between the Christian message and colonial treatment of Africans.

One such reformer was the American Joseph Booth, a fundamentalist missionary who came to Nyasaland in 1892 and soon saw the injustice of the system. In 1899 he wrote a letter to the British government denouncing colonial rule. This got him arrested and deported, but not before he had founded the African Christian Union, one of the first and most influential groups devoted to respect for African culture and the Pan-African ideal.

The first major religious uprising, and the only really effective rebellion against German colonial rule, occurred from 1905 to 1907 in Tanganyika, a part of German East Africa. Harsh taxation, forced labor, and cruel treatment had been sources of discontent among the native peoples for years, but there was not enough unity among them for any effective resistance to develop until a prophet emerged to bind them together. Preaching that their god had ordained a holy war against the Germans, Kinjikitile Ngwale promised his followers that in their fight for freedom German bullets would turn to water—*maji* in their language. Unfortunately, it didn't work; the bullets remained unchanged and found their marks, and the so-called Maji-Maji uprising failed. But it lasted nearly three years and introduced the idea of unity to the minds of many. It was Africa's first truly mass movement that included peoples of different tribes and locations, and it proved that by acting together they might accomplish something. Although the Germans suppressed the movement brutally, the Maji-Maji rebellion frightened them enough to make them reform some of their laws.

A few years later another religious rebellion in British-held Nyasaland had an even greater psychological effect among the Africans. One of Booth's converts, a young Yao named John Chilembwe, led an insurrection that became an inspiration for later independence movements. It was brief, and it never had the slightest chance of success, but it had an impact on African thought greater than many large-scale rebellions.

Under Booth's sponsorship, Chilembwe had attended a Baptist seminary in the United States. When he returned to Nyasaland in 1900 as a missionary, he was a good Christian and a loyal subject of the colony, but in time what he saw there disillusioned him. "By 1914," as

John Gailey wrote in his *History of Africa from 1800 to Present* (1972), "his position was that European colonial rule was a mockery of Christianity and that the only way that Africans could free themselves from European control was by force." His attempt to overthrow the government of Nyasaland was doomed from the beginning, but it reflected the desperation he and his followers felt. With an "army" of only a few hundred, he launched an attack that began and ended in 1915. His instructions to his men, now a classic in the literature of African independence, show how little hope he had of success, but they also show the larger vision that inspired him:

> You are all patriots as you sit. . . . This very night you are to go and strike the blow and then die. . . . This is the only way to show the whiteman that the treatment they are treating our men and women was most bad and we are determined to strike a first and a last blow and then die by the heavy storm of the whiteman's army. The whiteman will then think after we are dead that the treatment they are treating our people is almost bad, and they might change to the better for our people.

The revolt lasted less than a week. The rebels killed a few planters (touching neither their wives nor their property) and were soon rounded up. Chilembwe was killed after a brief chase, 40 of his men were hanged or executed by firing squads, and some 300 were imprisoned. But this short-lived uprising was not forgotten, and Chilembwe's words have echoed down through the years. As Gailey has written of his hopeless gesture, "It was the first nationalistic movement led by an African which had as its goal the idealistic motives of Christianity."

Other religious movements have entered the political field more gradually but have supported Africans' desire for independence in more direct ways. In 1921 a Congolese Protestant preacher, Simon Kimbangu, developed such a following that the Belgians considered him dangerous. He was arrested for "disrupting order" and sentenced to death, but the public outcry was so great the government agreed to spare his life and merely banish him. Although he was no longer available to lead it, his following increased. A sect named the Church of Jesus Christ on Earth by the Prophet Simon Kimbangu sprang up and spread beyond the borders of the colony, preaching the equality of the races and opposition to Belgian rule. It did not engage in open warfare like the Maji-Maji rebellion, but it was active in promoting the end of colonialism from the pulpit, and it engaged directly in Congolese politics in the 1950s. By the end of the next decade, it had established itself over so great an area and included such an extensive following (estimated at over 3 million) that it became a member of the World Council of Churches.

These early military and religious movements had little direct effect on African independence. None—except the opposition force in Ethiopia—ever repelled or ousted a colonial government. But even the smallest local uprising helped sustain the African desire for freedom, and the religious rebellions kept alive the flame of faith in spiritual independence. The resistance to invasion and the revolt against occupation that persisted from the beginnings of colonial times kept the African soil fertile for the return of self-government.

## WORLD WAR II

The call for independence remained sporadic and isolated for a long time in Africa. It was not until the Second World War that it found a focus and a unified direction. That international conflict was the turning point in the road to African liberation for several reasons.

First, the greatly increased demands for raw materials for the war brought about a great change in traditional patterns of life in Africa, and the old colonial methods of control became impossible to maintain. The rural economy was shattered as villagers were forced from their small farms into the cities to work for the war effort. Huge sprawling slums developed. It is estimated that the population of African cities tripled or quadrupled from 1939 to 1945. Africans of many ethnic groups began to live and work together and to exchange ideas. Organizations began to form for mutual support. At first they were based on ethnic groups, but soon these associations grew into political movements, replacing tribal and regional loyalties with a sense of national purpose.

A more important effect of the war came from the fact that when the fighting reached the shores of Africa, hundreds of thousands of Africans were drafted into the French and English armies. There too, as in the newly teeming cities, different groups were thrown together

## FROM *CAHIER D'UN RETOUR AU PAYS NATAL (NOTES ON A RETURN TO THE NATIVE LAND)*

A classic in the 20th-century African consciousness movement called "Négritude" (see the boxed feature on p. 32), this 1938 book-length poem in free verse by the Caribbean poet Aimé Césaire (1913– ) was the first to use the word in print.

> Listen to the white world,
> Horribly weary from its enormous effort,
> Its rebellious joints crack beneath the hard stars,
> Its rigid blue steel penetrates the mystic flesh;
> Hear its traitorous victories trumpet its defeats;
> Hear the grandiose alibis for its sorry stumblings,
> Pity for our conquerors, omniscient and naive! . . .
>
> And here at the end of dawn is my virile prayer,
> Eyes fixed on the beautiful city I prophesy:
> May I hear neither laughter nor cries,
> Give to my hands the power to mold,
> Give to my soul the temper of steel,
> I do not shrink. Make of my head a spearhead, and of my self,

to share their problems and complaints. Many saw action overseas and were able to observe the differences between their own poor lives and those of the relatively rich and free Europeans, and they realized for the first time just how oppressed they were. Returning home to their overcrowded urban ghettos or the desolate poverty of the countryside, limited to the most menial jobs when they could find any work at all, they grew even more dissatisfied. The West had brought education to Africa, and a new generation of well-informed Africans came to realize their rights. Protest and rebellion increased, and Europe, preoccupied with the war, did not have the money, arms, or manpower to suppress them.

> my heart, make not a father nor a brother, but *the* father,
> brother, son; not a husband but the lover of this single
> people;
> Make me rebel against all vanity but as docile to its genius,
> As the fist is to the arm;
> Make me the servant of its blood,
> The trustee of its resentment,
> Make of me a man who terminates,
> Make of me a man who initiates,
> Make of me a man who contemplates,
> But make of me as well a man who sows;
> Make me the executor of these lofty works,
> For now is the time to gird one's loins like a valiant man.
> But in doing so, my heart, preserve me from all hatred.
> Make not of me that man of hate
> For whom I've only hate. . . .
>
> For it is not true that the work of man is finished,
> That there is nothing for us to do in this world,
> That we are parasites on this earth,
> That it is enough for us to keep in step with the world,
> But the work of man has only just begun,
> And it is up to man to vanquish all deprivations . . .
> And no race has a monopoly on beauty, intelligence, or
> strength. . . .

In fact, Europe was beginning to reconsider the idea of empire. France and Belgium, occupied by Germans during the war, were unable to administer their colonies, and Great Britain found that its colonies had become a luxury it simply could not afford. Britain began making plans to free some of its colonies in Asia, such as India, Ceylon, and Burma, and the colonial subjects in Africa saw the possibility of gaining their own freedom.

And increasingly, they were not alone in their protest. World attention was drawn to the condition of the Africans, and public sentiment grew in their favor. The United States and the Soviet Union—both opposed to colonialism on principle—emerged as the major world powers, and both criticized Europe for its treatment of Africa. As Waldemar A. Neilsen has written, "Ideas of democracy and human rights had so penetrated European life . . . that the political foundations of colonialism had largely rotted away."

## THE ATLANTIC CHARTER

In 1941, the American president Franklin D. Roosevelt and the British prime minister Winston Churchill issued the Atlantic Charter. This was a document intended to rally support for the war, but it was later taken as a blueprint for the postwar world. In it the two statesmen called for "the right of all peoples to choose the form of government under which they will live." Great Britain did not intend the Atlantic Charter to be a promise to give up their empire, but many Africans took it for that and fully expected to be freed when the war ended. Some British people believed the same, although they didn't expect it to happen quite so soon. In 1945 a group of British colonial administrators wrote encouragingly in a report on African schools, "Somewhere in West Africa within a century, within half a century—and what is that in the life of a people—a new African state will be born."

## THE UNITED NATIONS

Africa was not freed when the war ended, but the pressure from within and without was gaining momentum. In 1945, the newly formed United Nations reaffirmed the principles of the Atlantic Charter in even stronger terms. In the preamble to its own charter, it asserts its "faith in the fundamental human rights, in the dignity and worth of men and women of nations large and small" and directs all nations with colonies "to develop self-government, to take due account of the political aspirations of the people, and to assist them in the progressive development of their free political institutions." The road to freedom would not be an easy one—not nearly as easy as the leaders of the new independence movements demanded—but the journey had begun.

## CHAPTER FIVE NOTES

p. 48    "Jesus, Savior . . ." Hymn from the Kimbanguist Church's *Chants du Ciel (Songs from Heaven)*, quoted in Thomas Hodgkin.

*Nationalism in Colonial Africa* (New York University Press, 1957), p. 111.

p. 50     "... the longest series of campaigns ..." A. Adu Boahen, ed. *Africa Under Colonial Domination 1880–1935* (Berkeley, Calif.: University of California Press, 1990), p. 63.

p. 50     "I have heard your words . . ." Yao chief Machemba, quoted in Robert I. Rotberg and Ali A. Mazrui. *Protest and Power in Black Africa* (New York: Oxford University Press, 1970), p. 74.

p. 51     "We are not able to pay for our houses. . . ." Letter from Timini Chiefs to District Commissioner William S. Sharpe, Sierra Leone, December 17, 1896, quoted in Rotberg and Mazrui, p. 182.

p. 54     "You are all patriots as you sit ..." George S. Mwase. *Strike a Blow and Die: A Narrative of Race Relation in Colonial Africa* (1931–32), ed. by Robert I. Rotberg, (Cambridge, England: Cambridge University Press, 1967), pp. 48–49.

p. 56     "Listen to the white world, . . ." Aimé Césaire, from *Notes on a Return to the Native Land*, 1938, quoted in Ellen Conroy Kennedy, ed. *The Negritude Poets* (New York: Thunder's Mouth Press, 1989), pp. 77–78.

p. 58     "Ideas of democracy and human rights ..." Waldemar A. Neilsen. *Africa* (New York: Atheneum, 1966), p. 15.

# INDEPENDENCE FOR THE BRITISH COLONIES

Africans who want self-government are always put off with:
"Not yet. Not till you are fit for it." Certainly we aspire to be
fit for self-government. But we should like to know who is
to be the judge of our fitness, and by what standard will his
verdict be pronounced?
                        —Jomo Kenyatta, Kenya, letter to the British
                        magazine *The Listener*, August, 1943

The end of colonial rule in Africa goes by different
names, according to who is talking about it. To the Africans it was
"independence" or "liberation," but the Europeans who held territories
on the continent often prefer to call it "decolonization" or "the transfer
of power." For the British, who had claimed, from the beginning of
colonization, that they were preparing the native peoples for self-government, the transition was generally peaceful, though sometimes
reluctant. The colonial governments began relinquishing some authority in their western colonies after World War II, allowing native

representation in the local legislatures and appointing a few Africans to minor offices. But real independence in Africa was seldom won without organized political agitation, if not bloodshed, even in the relatively liberal British colonies.

## EGYPT (1922)

The first of Great Britain's "spheres of influence" to attain independence was Egypt. Officially a self-governing part of the Turkish Empire since the 16th century, Egypt suddenly became the hub of trade between Europe, Asia, and Africa when the Suez Canal opened in 1869. Britain, the major maritime power of the age and a big investor in the canal, involved itself in Egyptian affairs and soon made itself an important, if indirect, political and economic power in the Nile Valley. When World War I broke out in 1914, Great Britain declared Egypt a protectorate, explaining as its reason the need to safeguard the Suez Canal from enemy attack.

Egypt profited from British protection and investment, but nationalist feeling had been growing during centuries of Turkish rule. As World War I progressed, that feeling grew stronger. In November 1918, two days after the Armistice that brought the war to an end, a delegation of Egyptian officials formally petitioned the British High Commissioner in Cairo for independence. This delegation was the beginning of a nationalist political party called Wafd—literally "delegation" in Arabic—which was the first true mass political party in Africa.

It appears that the British did not take the demands of this modest delegation very seriously, but the Wafd was not to be shrugged off. When its demands were ignored, it began organizing demonstrations and strikes. This led to the customary colonial response: All the leaders of the movement were arrested and imprisoned or deported. In the past, this had been enough to dampen the spirits of African nationalists, but with the end of Turkish rule there was a new passion for independence in Egypt. A proud, independent people conscious of their long and rich history, the Egyptians did not accept British force patiently. The arrests in 1919 led to other and more violent demonstrations. "In every corner, disorderly crowds gathered, terrorizing the executive and demonstrating when and where they pleased . . . ," according to one surprised British witness. "Anarchy prevailed in some places, self-appointed committees replaced government in others." The British, still recovering from the war, were in no condition to put down a full-scale rebellion, and they agreed to negotiate.

After two and a half years of ceaseless pressure from the Wafd, Great Britain surprised everyone by simply giving in. In 1922 it declared Egypt a free nation, although its agreement included keeping some financial authority and British troops were stationed to enforce that authority. It was less than a complete victory for the Wafd and Egyptian nationalism, but it was an opening wedge—and the first success of an independence movement on the continent.

Great Britain continued to exercise some authority in North Africa, where it had occupied Libya and shared control over the Sudan with Egypt until the 1950s, but by the middle of that decade it had effectively given up all claims to the region. It had maintained a military or economic presence there by treaty, but not a full colonial government, and when it withdrew, the transition was generally a smooth and peaceful one. In West Africa, however, the independence movements' demands for liberation were more complicated, involving complete reorganization of governments.

The British were prepared to give up power, and in their own leisurely way were preparing the native peoples to accept it, but they saw self-government as something for a distant future, after many generations had come and gone and the "primitive" Africans had been "civilized." If African intellectuals talked of "freedom now," the British smiled and counseled patience. By making small concessions to nationalist ambitions and local pride, they hoped to keep things under control without giving up any real power.

Pursuing a policy of "gradualism," Great Britain granted its West African colonies constitutions after World War II and allowed increasing representation in legislative councils. But it was too little and too late. The tide of nationalism had already begun, and the token gestures of independence the British offered were not enough. Well-organized and well-supported movements were already in place, and they demanded nothing less than total freedom.

## THE GOLD COAST (GHANA, 1957)

The breakthrough came in the Gold Coast, long a fertile ground for anticolonial feeling. The people of this area condemned the half-hearted constitution they were given in 1946 for providing the country with only the appearance of self-government. Although the constitution allowed an elected African majority in the government—a degree of representation never permitted before in a British colony in Africa—it kept control of the executive council in the hands of the British.

Profoundly dissatisfied with this constitution, nationalists in the Gold Coast formed an opposition group, led by London-educated lawyer and newspaper editor Joseph Danquah, in 1947. Called the United Gold Coast Convention (UGCC), it maintained pressure on the British government. Danquah had organized the Gold Coast Youth League in 1938 to discuss the problems of the colony, but the UGCC had more ambitious goals. It openly attacked the colonial government and proposed the organizing of another, under African control.

*Swazi dancers, Swaziland.* (Courtesy South African Consulate General, New York)

# KWAME NKRUMAH (1909–72)

The first African to head a post-colonial black government, Kwame Nkrumah led Ghana to independence in 1957 and became its first president. Although his policies were very controversial and he died in exile, his skill as a political organizer and his dedication to African independence and unity inspired many African leaders.

Nkrumah was born the son of a goldsmith in a small village in what was then the Gold Coast. Trained as a teacher, he was attracted to the nationalist cause, and at the age of 26 went to the United States to continue his studies. At Lincoln University in Pennsylvania and at the University of Pennsylvania, from both of which he received master's degrees, he was active in campus politics, organizing and leading the African Students' Association. In 1945 he moved to England, where he studied law at the London School of Economics and continued his political activities both on and off campus.

The head of the United Gold Coast Convention (UGCC), an African political party seeking national self-government,

*Kwame Nkrumah addresses the U.N., 1961.*   (Courtesy United Nations)

learned of Nkrumah's work and invited him to return to his country and become the organization's secretary-general in 1947. As a leader of the UGCC Nkrumah helped organize mass protest demonstrations and was imprisoned in 1948. Upon his release, he began to organize another, more radical group, the Convention People's Party (CPP), which demanded immediate independence from Great Britain for the Gold Coast, advocating a policy of "non-violence and non-cooperation—the adoption of all legitimate and constitutional means by which we can cripple the forces of imperialism in the country." Nkrumah was imprisoned again in 1951, but by that time his party had become so powerful that he was released to become a member of the Gold Coast's new legislative assembly. In 1952 he became the first African-born prime minister of a British colony. The Gold Coast gained its independence within the British Commonwealth, as Ghana, in 1957, with Nkrumah still prime minister. When it became a republic in 1960, Nkrumah was elected president.

Politically, Nkrumah was dedicated to what he called "Scientific Socialism," a system that included government control of industry. This and his dedication to the ideal of a united Africa angered many Ghanaians, who felt that the new nation would lose some of its freedom under such a system. Nkrumah became isolated from the public, assumed more and more power, and promoted a personality cult called "Nkrumaism." In 1964 he declared Ghana a one-party state and himself life-president.

Two years later, during a visit to Peking, Nkrumah was ousted from office by a military coup. President Sékou Touré of Guinea gave him asylum and declared him co-head of state, and while in exile he wrote some of his most important books on government. He never set foot in his country again, but when he died of cancer in 1972 he was buried with full honors in his native village.

Kwame Nkrumah inspired both love and hatred in Ghana. He was accused by some of being power-hungry and a communist, but others honored him as the hero who led the country to independence. A close friend of Martin Luther King Jr., Nkrumah was an African statesman with a vision that encompassed the whole continent.

The British responded with their usual lack of foresight by locking Dr. Danquah and his colleagues up, but once again it was too late. As in Egypt in 1922, jailing the leaders of the movement only increased public anger. In fact, this move hastened the end of British control in the Gold Coast more than the UGCC could have done if left alone. Danquah and his fellow organizers were moderate, middle-class people who had prospered under colonialism and might have accepted a gradual change in the government of the colony.

But whatever compromises might have been made in the governing of the Gold Coast, by 1947 things had passed the point of no return. In that year Danquah appointed a young man named Kwame Nkrumah as secretary-general of the UGCC. Nkrumah was a dynamic 38-year-old who had already built something of a name for himself as an African nationalist in the United States, where he had gone to college, and in Great Britain, where he had received his law degree and participated in the famous 1945 Pan-African Congress. Danquah and his colleagues recognized that this young firebrand had the personality and the dedication to spark some action. Deeply influenced by such New World thinkers as W. E. B. Du Bois and inspired by the dream of "Black nationalism" of Marcus Garvey, Nkrumah was fired with enthusiasm to make changes in the condition of his country. His selection for the post of secretary-general—really the leader—of UGCC was a decision that changed the course of African history.

Far more radical than Danquah and his fellow movement leaders, Nkrumah proceeded at once to reorganize the UGCC and widen its base of operation. His personal flair and his appeal to the young activated the group and molded it into a powerful protest movement. He led successful demonstrations and boycotts against European goods in 1948, and in 1949, impatient with the UGCC's moderation, left it to found his own movement, the more revolutionary Convention People's Party (CPP). As the voice of the CPP, he demanded "full independence now." The general strike he organized in 1950 led to violence and earned him a prison sentence, but it also forced the British to rewrite the constitution to allow an African majority not only in the legislature but in the executive council.

The CPP won the election of 1951, and Nkrumah emerged from his cell to become prime minister of the first native government in colonial

Africa. Nkrumah and the CPP pressed for full independence, and the British, seeing the advantage of retaining cordial relations with a former colony, agreed to allow the Gold Coast to decide its own political fate by vote. The people of the colony unhesitatingly elected the CPP to govern them. In 1957, the Gold Coast renamed itself Ghana and became a sovereign nation, the first European colony in Africa to achieve independence through its own efforts.

Ghana's peaceful emergence, after 137 years as a British colony, has been described as "the gentle beginning of the powerful Black Nationalist Revolution that was to sweep across Africa." In the next few years, Great Britain and the other colonizing nations of Europe were to give up, more or less willingly, almost all their holdings in Africa.

## NIGERIA (1960)

More than three times as big and six times as populous as Ghana, its nearest neighbor held by Great Britain in West Africa, Nigeria had special problems in seeking independence. One of the principal difficulties in organizing independence movements in Africa was the tribal and regional diversity within the European colonies, and Nigeria was more deeply divided than most. Unlike the relatively unified Ghana, Nigeria was an artificially created nation populated by unrelated and hostile peoples. The Muslim north was governed as a separate territory until 1946, and in southern Nigeria the east and west were deeply divided. These cultural and economic divisions delayed the drive for independence because people could not agree on a course of action. Some wanted a unified nation with a single government, others argued for a federation of states, and a few believed in forming three separate nations.

There were native political parties in Nigeria as early as the 1920s, but no dominant movement that represented the entire colony existed until the coming of World War II generated a desire for national independence. One young soldier, drafted into England's army to serve in India, spoke for all Nigerians when he wrote in a letter, "We all overseas soldiers are coming back home with new ideas. We have been taught what we fought for. That is 'freedom.' We want freedom, nothing but freedom." In 1944 the American-educated journalist

Nnamdi Azikiwe formed the first party that tried to rise above ethnic and regional boundaries, the National Council of Nigeria and Cameroons (NCNC), but its main support came from the Ibo people in the east. In 1949 the Northern Peoples Congress (NPC) arose in the Fulani- and Hausa-dominated north. Two years later, the Action Group (AG) was formed among the Yoruba who dominated the west.

Although these three groups were in some ways rivals, each supporting its own region above the national interest, they all agreed on the goal of "self-government by 1956," and if it had not been for the quarrels among them, they might have achieved it. Eventually they reached enough of an agreement to vote Nigeria an independent nation in 1960, sharing its government among the three parties.

## EASTERN AFRICA

The region in which the Pan-African movement concentrated its efforts and from which its principal African members came, West Africa was the first sub-Saharan region to press home its demands for independence. But the fever for freedom was not long in spreading. The influence of the movement was also felt in the rich colony of Tanganyika (now a part of Tanzania) on the east coast, where Julius Nyerere formed a powerful party called Tanganyika African National Union (TANU). Following Nkrumah's model, he organized strikes and riots that forced Great Britain to surrender in 1961.

The turning point in the liberation of British East Africa came with the independence of Kenya in 1963. Perhaps no British colony was given up so unwillingly, or after longer and more desperate pressure, than this large, prosperous land. The history of open, organized protest in Kenya goes back to 1920, when the Kikuyu Association was formed in the capital, Nairobi, to protest British appropriation of tribal lands. The next year Harry Thuku, "the father of Kenya's political consciousness," founded the Young Kikuyu Association and the multitribal East African Association (EAA).

When Thuku was arrested on charges of being "dangerous to peace and good order," the effect was explosive. Huge demonstrations demanded his release. Both sexes and all ages participated in these protests. In one, the women began taunting the men for holding back. A witness reported

Mary Nyanjiru leapt to her feet, pulled her dress right up over her shoulders and shouted to the men: "You take my dress and give me your trousers. You men are cowards. What are you waiting for? Our leader is in there. Let's get him." Mary and the others pushed on until the bayonets . . . were pricking at their throats, and then the firing started. Mary was one of the first to die.

Settlers and militia together began shooting into the unarmed crowd, killing 56 men, women, and children.

The EAA was officially disbanded by government order in 1925, but reborn immediately as the Kikuyu Central Association (KCA), which operated as the only effective voice of the largest tribe in Kenya. When the KCA was banned in 1940, it shed its tribal identification and reappeared as the country's first really national movement, the Kenya African Union (KAU), (which everyone pronounced "cow").

*Jomo Kenyatta, president of Kenya, at a meeting of the Economic Commission for Africa, 1965. A member of his country's majority Kikuyu tribe, Kenyatta wears a cap from the rival Luo as a public sign of his government's impartiality.* (Courtesy United Nations 88920 JH/ME)

## MAU MAU

Of all the independence movements in Africa, perhaps none was so directly effective as the mysterious Kenyan secret society known as *Mau Mau*. Consisting mainly of members of the Kikuyu tribe, the largest in Kenya, Mau Mau was a terrorist group whose origins remain unknown. In fact, no one even knows what the name means. Some think it was an imitation of a lion's roar; others say it came from the initial letters of the words of a Kikuyu motto meaning "Let the Europeans return to England" or a rearrangement of the letters of *uma uma*, Kikuyu for "get out."

The British first became aware of Mau Mau in 1948, and its first mention in newspapers appeared in 1950. People were unsure what it was at first. Some thought it was a religious movement, a political party, or even a communist unit sponsored by the Soviet Union. But it soon became clear that its sole objective was to drive the Europeans out of Kenya and restore control of the land to the Africans.

At secret ceremonies deep in the forest, Mau Mau's members took oaths to kill whites and any blacks who collaborated with them. Mau Mau's victims were often horribly mutilated. Many Kikuyu opposed these means of gaining freedom and refused to participate in Mau Mau, but it has been estimated that as many as 90 percent of the tribe belonged to it by 1951.

The British used many methods to defeat the terrorists. They flew in 11 infantry battalions from England, assigned 21,000 policemen to the fight, and established a "Home Guard" of 25,000 men. They bombed villages thought to be Mau Mau strongholds and interned some 80,000 Kikuyu in

Active in protest movements since he joined the EAA in 1922 was a Kikuyu named Jomo Kenyatta, who became general secretary of the KCA in 1928 and president of the KAU in 1947. An eloquent speaker and a shrewd tactician, Kenyatta led the movement until it was banned in 1953, and again when it reappeared in 1957 renamed the Kenya African National Union (KANU) to emphasize its nationalist goals.

concentration camps, where many died. In 1952 the colonial government declared a state of emergency and arrested the nationalist leader Jomo Kenyatta, head of the Kenya African Union (KAU) and later the first president of the country, on suspicion of "managing Mau Mau." Kenyatta spent nine years in prison.

It took the colonial government until 1956 to break up Mau Mau, and the cost was tremendous in both money and international respect. In 1955–56, almost 50 percent of the national budget of Kenya was spent on prisons and police. During all the years of national "emergency," Mau Mau took the lives of only 32 white civilians and 167 security officers, while the British killed 11,503 guerrillas in battle and hanged more than 1,000. What the colonial government learned from this bitter experience was that white Kenyans could never maintain control of the country on their own. The British accepted the necessity of political reform and agreed to let Africans own land in rural areas. In 1960 it consented to an elected African majority in the legislative council, the first step toward national independence.

There are different opinions on whether Mau Mau helped or hurt African political progress in Kenya. Some see the guerrillas as freedom fighters, while others think they delayed the peaceful settlement of political problems. Certainly the terrible conflict they maintained cost many lives and postponed negotiations. But without the persistent pressure of Mau Mau, the entrenched white settlers of Kenya would probably never have consented to the reforms that led to independence.

The British finally realized in the mid-1950s that it was impossible to quench Kenya's will for independence, and it grudgingly began to allow African representation in its legislative and executive councils. In 1963 Kenya was granted internal self- government, the first step to full independence. KANU won a large majority in the general election, and Jomo Kenyatta became president when Kenya became an independent republic later in the year.

## "AFRICA IS FAST AWAKENING . . ."

Our objective here in Africa is justice, after long years of desolation, exploitation and neglect. Africa is fast awakening, not for conquest or disruption or revenge, but to contribute to the world a new philosophy. All men are equal. All men are equally entitled to respect. The talents and resources of the world are enough to banish squalor, and to bridge the gap between the richer nations and those where poverty has stifled man's creativeness.

—Jomo Kenyatta

Although Nyasaland (now Malawi) had been the scene of John Chilembwe's tragic uprising in 1916, the pressure for national independence in that desperately poor territory in South-Central Africa was not strong until the 1950s because the region had little contact with the outside world. The 3 million native peoples there were not much affected by the 5,000 whites living among them, and there were issues more important to them than their oppression by the English. It took the threat of federation with the strongly white-dominated colonies of Northern and Southern Rhodesia to awaken a desire for independence. When those two potentially rich colonies joined together and incorporated Nyasaland into the Central African Federation in 1953, the people of Nyasaland knew they would be used as a source of cheap labor for Rhodesian mines and factories, and that they would lose what little national identity they had.

A group of teachers and clerks had formed the Nyasaland African Congress (NAC) in 1944, but it had asked for nothing more than some educational reforms and minor political concessions. Now it woke up to Nyasaland's need to escape, not only from the Central African Federation but from British colonial control. A song inspired by Karl Marx's revolutionary writings became their anthem:

> Men of Nyasa, Unite! Unite!
> You have nothing to lose but your chains.
> Join up, Join up and Fight the Good Fight
> And Freedom shall be the least of your gains.

The Central African Federation was just as racist as the Nyasa people feared it would be. Its all-white government ruled the huge African majority with an iron hand. The NAC had almost no support until it was taken over by a Nyasa physician named Hastings Banda, who returned from his medical practice in Ghana to "Fight the Good Fight" with his compatriots in 1958. Banda had been keenly aware of the dangers of the federation since the 1940s, when he and a fellow nationalist wrote from England,

> Of all the Europeans of Central Africa, those of Southern Rhodesia have the worst antipathy towards Africans. . . . They look upon the Africans as inferior beings, with no right to a dignified and refined existence and fit only as hewers of wood and drawers of water for Europeans. . . . Under the government provided by Southern Rhodesia, the relationship between us and the authorities will be one of slaves and masters.

Banda's prediction proved correct, and he led the NAC in protesting the federation until his party was banned in 1959. Like most independence leaders in British colonies, he was sent to prison, but he returned to his antifederation speeches at the head of the newly formed Malawi Congress Party (MCP) when he was released in 1960. In time the demonstrations he organized had their effect. The Central African Federation was disbanded in 1963, and Nyasaland, renamed Malawi for the 17th-century empire, became a republic in 1964 with Dr. Banda as its president.

The African majority in Northern Rhodesia was as unhappy about the federation as the Nyasas because their labor was equally exploited. Kenneth Kaunda, the schoolteacher son of an African Christian missionary, led the United National Independence Party (UNIP) in modest demands for the right of Africans to vote. A skilled organizer who mobilized the masses to coordinate a broad base for the movement, Kaunda had profited from the ideas of the Pan-Africanists and knew the importance of unity. Putting aside all tribal and regional conflicts, he worked together with Banda's MCP and nationalist parties in Southern Rhodesia. "The white man lords it over us . . . not because he happens to be white," Kaunda wrote, "but because he is better organized; that is his secret."

Using that secret to good advantage, Kaunda organized UNIP along the lines of a European political party, and with the slogan *Kwacha*— "the dawn"—it won a large popular vote in the 1962 regional legislative elections. Known as Africa's "gentle rebel," Kaunda continued to steer his country without violence toward self-government. Three months after the independence of Malawi (they dropped the hated name of Rhodesia, which recalled Cecil Rhodes, the white leader who had taken their land), the new republic of Zambia, named for the Zambesi River, was proclaimed.

## GAMBIA (1965)

The smallest of Great Britain's possessions, Gambia was its first African territory. It was occupied as early as 1588 and became an official British possession in 1843. A tiny strip surrounded on three sides by the French

*Kenneth D. Kaunda, president of Zambia, at a U.N. press conference, 1989.* (Courtesy United Nations 175322 J. Isaac)

colony of Senegal along the banks of the Gambia River, it made no real effort to establish itself as a sovereign nation, and its People's Progressive Party (PPP) did little more than defend the colony from absorption by Senegal. But in the wave of independence sweeping through Africa, it was given its freedom in 1965, more by the will of its British administrators than by any political pressure of its own, and added "The" to its name, becoming officially The Gambia. With the independence of The Gambia, Britain surrendered its last territorial claim in West Africa.

## SOUTHERN RHODESIA (ZIMBABWE, 1980)

Britain had almost dismantled its colonial system by 1975, when it gave up the 115 small Seychelle islands in the Indian Ocean. It had only one remaining possession in Africa, Southern Rhodesia. The last outpost of British rule on the continent, and the last European colony to achieve independence, Southern Rhodesia (known simply as Rhodesia after Northern Rhodesia won its independence as Zambia in 1964) has a complex history unlike that of any other colony in Africa.

Opposition to white rule in the area dates back to the 19th century, when local uprisings were frequent. A clearly defined movement for national independence in Southern Rhodesia began to form during the same period as in Nyasaland and Northern Rhodesia, when the threat of inclusion in the racist Central African Federation prompted the same fears of exploitation among its native peoples. When the Central African Federation was dissolved in 1963 and its two other members given their independence the next year, the nationalists of Southern Rhodesia demanded their own, and guerrilla attacks began. The two major parties, the Zimbabwe National People's Union (ZAPU) and its rival, the more militant Zimbabwe African National Union (ZANU), both named for the great empire that had flourished in the area from the 15th to the 18th century, were backed by rival ethnic groups and were often in conflict, but they agreed in wanting the British out of their country. The white minority—they comprised about 250,000 out of a total population of over 7.5 million—were just as determined not to give in.

What is unusual about the colonial history of Rhodesia is that the white settlers campaigned and demonstrated for independence no less than the Africans did. The British, by now anxious to end their ruinous efforts at maintaining a presence in Africa, were more than willing to give Rhodesia up but refused to grant independence to a colony whose government was not representative of the entire population. A conservative white-supremacist party, the only white independence movement in the history of the continent, formed to oppose the African majority rule demanded by Britain as a condition of independence. Named the Rhodesian Front (RF), it argued that the white population of Rhodesia represented the forces of "civilization" against those of "barbarism" and that political power could not be entrusted to the "uncivilized."

Rhodesia and Great Britain negotiated, but Great Britain's demands for African voting and political rights were unacceptable to the colony's white government. With ZAPU and ZANU both banned, their leaders silenced, the newspapers censored, and some concessions made to native chiefs, the Rhodesian government tried to convince Great Britain that there was no further African opposition to independence with a white government in charge. But the British were not convinced and continued to refuse. At last, in 1965, the Rhodesian prime minister, Ian Smith, concluded that his country and Great Britain would never come to terms. He declared Rhodesia independent himself, issuing what he called a Unilateral Declaration of Independence (UDI). It was patterned very closely on the document with which the United States had declared itself free of Britain in 1776, and Smith tried to present Rhodesia's situation as similar to that of the heroic American colonists nearly 200 years before. In his independence message to his people, Smith proclaimed, "We Rhodesians have rejected the doctrinaire philosophy of appeasement and surrender. . . . We have struck a blow for the preservation of justice, civilization and Christianity."

Smith's argument didn't satisfy anyone but the white Rhodesians themselves. Great Britain simply rejected the declaration, and neither the United Nations nor any country in the world recognized the independence of Rhodesia. The only support the white government had was from South Africa and the Portuguese colonies of Mozambique and Angola, hoping to maintain a line between the black north and the white-ruled south on the continent.

ZAPU and ZANU, now both illegal, went underground and established bases in sympathetic neighboring countries. A military arm of

ZAPU, the Zimbabwe People's Revolutionary Army (ZIPRA), prepared for war, and guerrilla attacks became frequent, supported with both sympathy and actual military help from outside. By the middle 1970s, a state of war existed. The U.S.S.R. and Communist China supplied arms and training to the anticolonial movements, and the United States, alarmed by the growing communist influence in southern Africa, added its voice to the demand for majority rule in Rhodesia. When Mozambique and Angola gained their independence from Portugal in 1974 and 1975, white Rhodesia lost two allies. Isolated internationally and torn by a ruinous war, it was finally forced to consent to a constitution that granted full voting rights to the African majority. Although there was no unified independence movement among the divided African community, it was clear that white rule had come to an end in Rhodesia.

Elections under the new constitution were held in 1979 and established an African government. With huge relief, Great Britain declared the last of its African colonies, renamed Zimbabwe, independent in 1980.


## CHAPTER SIX NOTES

p. 60     "Africans who want self-government . . ." Jomo Kenyatta, letter to the British magazine *The Listener*, August, 1943.

pp. 61–62 "In every corner, disorderly crowds gathered . . ." Quoted in Robin Hallett. *Africa Since 1875* (Ann Arbor, Mich.: University of Michigan Press, 1974), p. 137.

p. 67     "We all overseas soldiers . . ." Theo Ayoola, in a letter quoted in Sanford J. Ungar. *Africa* (New York: Simon & Schuster, 1989), p. 125.

p. 69     "Mary Nyanjiru leapt to her feet . . ." Quoted in Dennis Wepman. *Jomo Kenyatta* (New York: Chelsea House, 1985), pp. 40–41.

p. 72     "Our objective here in Africa . . ." Jomo Kenyatta, in Wepman, p. 83.

p. 72     "Men of Nyasa, Unite! Unite! . . ." Quoted in Hallett, p. 532.

p. 73     "Of all the Europeans of Central Africa . . ." Hastings Banda and Harry Nkumbula, in a memorandum to the British government dated May 1949, quoted in Robert I. Rotberg. *The Rise of Nationalism in Central Africa: The Making of Malawi and Zambia* (Cambridge, Mass.: Harvard University Press, 1964), p. 224.

p. 73    "The white man lords it over us . . ." Kenneth D. Kaunda. *Zambia Shall Be Free: An Autobiography* (London: Heinemann, 1962), p. 152.

p. 76    "We Rhodesians have rejected . . ." Quoted in Martin Meredith. *The First Dance of Freedom: Black Africa in the Post-War Era* (New York: Harper and Row, 1984), p. 172.

---

# SOUTH AFRICA
# AND SOUTH-
# WEST AFRICA

---

*We, the People of South Africa, declare to all our country
and the world to know:*
that South Africa belongs to all who live in it, black and
white, and that no government can justly claim authority
unless it is based on the will of the people.
> —Freedom Charter of the National Council
> of the Congress of the People, South Africa,
> 1963

The history of colonization and liberation in South
Africa and South-West Africa (Namibia) is different from that of any
other country in Africa, and its last chapter has yet to be written. South
Africa is a sovereign nation—that is, it is not a colony governed by
another country—but it nevertheless has its own independence movements. They are not seeking national independence, as the British
colonies did in the 1950s and 1960s, but rather liberation for the
population from an oppressive white minority government.

---

The status of South-West Africa—a German colony from 1885 to 1914, a protectorate of South Africa from 1914 to 1945, and under South Africa's unofficial domination until 1990—was the last to be defined. South Africa defiantly continued to administer it as a colony until it was forced to relinquish it. Today South Africa remains the last remnant of white-dominated Africa.

## SOUTH AFRICA

The southern tip of the continent has been under the control of Europeans or their descendants since the establishment of a settlement by the Dutch in Cape Town in 1652, a few years after the British founded their first colonies in the New World. The British conquered the Dutch colony in 1806, wanting it for a provisioning station for their ships at the half-way point in their voyages to India, and declared it a British colony in 1814. The new government introduced laws protecting the rights of the native population, abolishing slavery in 1833. The Dutch-descended settlers, known as Boers ("farmers" in their language), were to accommodate to the British policies. Slaves were an important part of the Boer work force. As the missionary-explorer David Livingstone wrote in 1857,

> The great objection many of the Boers had, and still have, to English law is that it makes no distinction between black men and white. They felt aggrieved by their supposed losses in the emancipation of their Hottentot slaves, and determined to erect themselves into a republic, in which they might pursue without molestation the "proper treatment" of the blacks. It is almost needless to add that the "proper treatment" has always contained in it the essential element of slavery namely compulsory labour.

For that purpose, the Boers began to migrate into the interior in search of land to form a new settlement. They easily crushed all native opposition on the way and created two independent republics (the Orange Free State and Transvaal) north and east of Britain's Cape Colony. The British established their own settlements in the region, and the two European groups lived side by side in relative peace—until

*Zulu mine dancers, South Africa.* (Courtesy South African Consulate General, New York)

gold was discovered in 1867 and diamonds in 1886, both in Boer territory.

The struggles for control that resulted finally led to the Boer War of 1899–1902. The Boers, who by then preferred to call themselves Afrikaners, fought valiantly, but their determination was no match for British military strength, and the entire southern territory became a British territory in 1910 as the Union of South Africa. Although under British control, this union of white settlers was permitted to establish its own administration, which effectively excluded the native population of southern Africa from economic advancement or participation in government. The Afrikaner-led colony was given its official independence in 1931 and became an equal member of the British Commonwealth.

The white government's policy of enforced racial segregation, called apartheid, regulated every phase of South African life. It denied nonwhites the vote, forbade interracial marriage, required that Africans carry identification passes, and reserved most skilled jobs for the white minority. Black Africans were not permitted outside their home areas after certain hours, and their schools received barely one-tenth of the funding spent on education for the white minority. In 1959 the South African government established separate African states, called *bantustans* or homelands, within its borders to isolate the original inhabitants of the country still farther. These scattered reserves, internally self-governing but completely under the control of the national government, occupy only 13 percent of the land but contain almost 70 percent of the black population.

Opposition to apartheid has existed, even among some whites, both within the country and internationally, since before it was enacted into law during the 1940s and 1950s. At the first Pan-African Conference, in 1900, apartheid was already being denounced as a set of "vile principles." South Africa has been barred from many world organizations, such as the International Olympic Committee, because it has refused to select its representatives with racial equality. In 1961, Great Britain challenged South Africa's policy of apartheid because newly independent African states refused to join the Commonwealth while it contained a member with such laws. South Africa responded by withdrawing from the Commonwealth.

Although small local groups protesting racial discrimination have come and gone for centuries in South Africa, the first to be organized on a national scale was the National Native Congress (NNC), formed in 1912 and renamed the African National Congress (ANC) in 1923. Originally a moderate organization, the ANC became the leading voice for political and social reform in South Africa, and by the middle 1950s had attained worldwide recognition, serving as a model and an inspiration for independence movements in many emerging African nations. Although it has rivals, it remains the best-known and most trusted opposition group in the country.

In 1952 the ANC organized its first major campaign to protest the humiliating "pass" laws under which more than 600,000 Africans a year were jailed in the 1950s for appearing on the streets without the required identification. Inspired by the methods of Mohandas K. Gandhi, who had protested the discrimination against East Indians in

South Africa years before, the ANC followed a policy of nonviolence, deliberately defying the pass laws and employing passive resistance when confronted by the police. The head of the African National Congress was Chief Albert Luthuli, whose moderation and opposition to violence had already earned him an international reputation and, in 1961, brought him the Nobel Peace Prize.

The South African government's response to the demonstrations was typical: It arrested many ANC leaders, including Luthuli, who was restricted to a remote farm and barred from writing for publication, speaking at public meetings, and even attending church services, for the rest of his life.

As peaceful protests continued to fail, independence movements of a more militant nature grew in South Africa. In 1959 the Pan-African Congress (PAC) was formed by Robert Sobukwe, inspired in part by the writings of W. E. B. Du Bois and Marcus Garvey on the need for unity. The PAC mobilized the entire black majority in a nationwide protest, and in 1960 it organized demonstrations in several cities in South Africa. The South African army broke up the meeting in Cape Town, but another in Sharpeville, near Johannesburg, so alarmed the police that they opened fire on the unarmed crowd, killing 69 people and wounding another 180. Newspapers all over the world attacked South Africa for its harshness and the injustice of its laws, but without effect. The government declared a state of emergency and passed a law enabling the police to hold people for successive 90-day periods without charges. More than 22,000 people were arrested, and Sobukwe was imprisoned indefinitely. Four years later, the ANC leader Nelson Mandela was sent to the same prison for organizing sabotage action, and the ANC was banned.

The effect of banning the ANC was to drive it underground and lead it to establish branches in other countries, links with foreign independence movements, and a military division, Umkhonto we Sizwe (Spear of the Nation), trained and equipped for sabotage and prepared for full-scale war.

In fact, however, the goal of the African National Congress and the other independence movements of South Africa has not been to take over the country, by war or by politics, but rather to achieve the rights of which blacks have been deprived by the white minority. When the

## ALBERT LUTHULI (1898–1967)

One of the pioneers of the liberation movement in South Africa, Albert Luthuli was a tribal chief and political organizer whose high principles and moderate philosophy helped shape modern African thought. Although he held no office and was silenced by law during the last 15 years of his life, he remained one of the most influential figures in South African life.

Luthuli was born in Southern Rhodesia (now Zimbabwe) and grew up in South Africa, where he studied at a Christian mission school and later taught at a mission college. The nephew of a Zulu chief, he was himself elected to a chieftainship when he was 38 years old. His administration of his tribe made him increasingly aware of the injustices suffered by the black population of the country and led to his joining the African National Congress (ANC), a political action group seeking racial justice. In 1952 he helped organize a "defiance campaign" in which thousands of Africans protested racial segregation in libraries, post offices, railway stations, and other public places by sit-in demonstrations. When he refused to call off the campaign, he was arrested, stripped of his chieftainship, and barred from visiting any of the major cities of the country.

His tribe responded by refusing to elect anyone to take his place as chief, and the ANC named him national president of

communist-inspired League of African Rights, formed in the 1920s, proposed a struggle for an independent "Native Republic," it was overwhelmingly rejected. As the Pan-Africanist George Padmore wrote of the idea, "Africans had never demanded any such nonsense . . . They, like the Negroes in America, while opposed to all forms of racial disability have never demanded separatism, either in the form of Apartheid or 'Native Republic.' Rather, the Africans have always demanded full citizenship rights within a multi-racial society."

The progress of black South Africans toward full citizenship rights has been almost imperceptible until recently. Under pressures from the organization. Determined to silence him, the South African government restricted him to his small farm and banned him from attending any public gatherings, but his influence remained great.

Chief Luthuli favored passive resistance, calling for work stoppages and economic boycotts to exert pressure on the racist government of his country. In recognition of his efforts, he was awarded the Nobel Peace Prize in 1961 because, as the announcement stated, "in his fight against racial discrimination he had always worked for nonviolent methods." The South African government condemned the award but could not prevent him from going to pick it up because of the pressure of world opinion. Until the day he left, and immediately after he returned, he was confined to his farm. There he lived in a five-room tin and concrete cottage that he had built himself at the end of an unpaved road. In 1967 he was killed by a train while crossing the tracks that ran by his field.

Despite the harsh treatment he received, Albert Luthuli never lost the faith and tolerance that made him an inspiration to political reformers around the world. "I have spent more than 30 years of my life patiently and politely knocking at a closed and barred door," he once said. But he was not discouraged from working for justice, believing, as he put it, that "South Africa is large enough to accommodate all people if they have large enough hearts."

without and within, the government made a few trifling concessions during the 1960s, but no substantial changes in the fundamental racism of its social and economic policies. Sixteen years after Sharpeville, in 1976, a peaceful demonstration of young students in the Johannesburg suburb of Soweto against the use of the Dutch-derived language Afrikaans instead of English in the schools brought about a repetition of the tragic event at Sharpeville. The police panicked when they saw the size of the group and began gunning down the children, firing volley after volley into the fleeing crowd. This set off a wave of riots, strikes, and protest marches throughout the country. The police responded

*A crowd of Zulus armed with spears, shields, and other weapons in a show of strength in the black Johannesburg suburb of Soweto, 1991.* (Courtesy AP/Wide World)

with equal violence, firing on unarmed demonstrators. By 1977, the death toll had been estimated at 1,500, and over 20,000 people were imprisoned for involvement in the "uprising." Again newspapers all over the world expressed outrage, and again the South African government seemed supremely indifferent to world opinion.

It was not until 1989 that a glimmer of light appeared on the South African horizon. Because of the sudden illness of the inflexible president P. W. Botha, who had resisted all change in his country's laws, the conservative National Party leader F. W. de Klerk assumed the office and surprised the world by making some substantial reforms in the racial policies of the country. Although all organized opposition was illegal, pressure from the oppressed majority continued, and the threat of revolution was in the air. Underground movements challenged the government, and de Klerk recognized that total white power could not be sustained in South Africa. He began, less than a month after his election, by releasing several imprisoned black leaders. Four months later, in February 1990, he legalized the ANC, the PAC, and the South African Communist Party, all long banned, and freed Nelson Mandela.

Within the next year de Klerk made several other major changes in South Africa's laws, and negotiations began for a new constitution extending equal political rights to all racial groups. Mandela, restored after many years in prison to the leadership of the ANC, became the principal negotiator for the black majority. In March 1992, the world

*Zulu woman with a beaded headdress, Natal, South Africa.* (Courtesy South African Consulate General, New York)

was amazed to read that a public vote of whites had granted de Klerk the support required to institute further reforms. Amid much uncertainty and dispute, apartheid—the principal cause of dissent in South Africa—appeared to be crumbling at last. No one expects a quick solution to the many problems of the country, but the process of power sharing has begun, and with it the long-overdue restoration of human rights to South Africa's racial majority.

## SOUTH-WEST AFRICA (NAMIBIA)

The scene of some of the worst atrocities in Africa's colonial history, South-West Africa remained without clear political identity for almost half a century. As a German colony it suffered the methodical slaughter of over 60,000 Herero men, women, and children, in retaliation for an uprising over German theft of the tribe's cattle in 1904. Following Germany's loss of its colonies after World War I, the territory was shamelessly exploited by South Africa, which had been assigned by the League of Nations to administer it. South Africa saw the assignment as the first step toward annexation of the territory. South African rule of South-West Africa included all the features of apartheid that have produced such tensions at home. Despite the League of Nations order to prepare the territory for self-government, South Africa treated South-West Africa as a colony and ruthlessly suppressed any protest. When the United Nations attempted to make South Africa fulfill the conditions of its assignment in 1945, South Africa simply refused. Like the League, the UN has been powerless to force South Africa to comply. In 1966 the UN terminated South Africa's mandate in South-West Africa and two years later officially recognized South-West Africa's government in exile and approved the change of its name to Namibia, but Pretoria continued to regard the region as a colony of South Africa and use its colonial name.

Among the many nationalist groups that have emerged and been crushed since the days of German occupation, only two have survived for more than a few years. The Ovambo people created the Ovamboland People's Congress, which became the South-West Africa People's Organization (SWAPO), and the Herero tribe launched the South-West Africa National Union (SWANU), both in 1959. More than three decades of fighting between both of these groups and the well-equipped and well-trained South African army produced few results except endless harsh reprisals. As the *Namibia News* noted bitterly in 1969,

> Guerrilla activities lead to mass-arrests, detentions of innocent civilians, brutal retaliation and victimization of the Namibian population. . . . The atrocities performed by the South African Government are as brutal and inhuman as those performed by Hitler's henchmen. . . . performed . . . in a part of the world where people happen to be black, happen to be exploited victims of international indifference.

Fierce resistance to South Africa's occupation of South-West Africa continued throughout the 1970s and 1980s. Although the UN had declared SWAPO "the sole authentic representative of the Namibian people," South Africa persisted in regarding the territory as its colony until 1989, when international pressure finally succeeded in bringing about popular elections there. On March 21, 1990, Namibia—the last colony on the continent—achieved its independence.

## CHAPTER SEVEN NOTES

p. 79    *"We the people of South Africa, . . ."* Freedom Charter of the National Council of the Congress of the People, South Africa, 1963, quoted in Mary Benson. *The Struggle for a Birthright* (Hammondsworth, England: Penguin, 1966), p. 160.

p. 80    "The great objection many of the Boers had . . ." David Livingstone. *Missionary Travels and Researches in South Africa,* 1857, quoted in Richard Gibson. *African Liberation Movements* (New York: Oxford University Press, 1972), p. 28.

p. 84    "Africans had never demanded any such nonsense . . ." George Padmore. *Pan-Africanism or Communism?* (London: Dobson, 1956), p. 351.

p. 89    "Guerrilla activities lead to mass-arrests, . . ." *Namibia News,* July/December 1969, quoted in Gibson, p. 133.

# INDEPENDENCE FOR THE FRENCH COLONIES

The colonial achievement in the Maghrib [Northwest Africa, comprising Morocco, Algeria, and Tunisia] was not intended for, and only indirectly affected, the welfare of the country itself. Exploitation may have been frequently judicious and sometimes even benevolent, but it was always focused on unilateral advantage.

> —Jacques Berque in his *French North Africa: The Maghrib Between the Two World Wars* (1967)

The liberation of the French territories in Africa took a different form from that of the British, because France saw itself as preparing its colonies for incorporation into France rather than for independence. Even before World War II, the name of the Ministry for Colonies of the French government was changed to the Ministry for France Overseas. The individual territories were to become departments, and its residents citizens, of France. One result of this "assimilationist" philosophy was that although there was frequent protest, there were fewer true independence movements among the French colonies. The organizations that formed to oppose the French colonial governments were concerned rather with making it easier for Africans to share in the benefits of European culture and attain the rights of French citizens than with achieving national independence.

Even so, the gathering momentum of the independence movements among the British colonies in Africa led the French territories to demand increased rights, if not total independence, and France accepted the fact that it would have to make some concessions. In 1941, when France fell to the Germans, the African colonies supported it heroically. Africa's contribution to the Free French cause was essential to General Charles de Gaulle's war efforts, and the French government in exile recognized that this loyalty earned the colonies the reward of a greater degree of self-government.

In 1944, General de Gaulle called a meeting in Brazzaville, the capital of what was then called Middle Congo (now simply Congo) and of the larger colonial territory of French Equatorial Africa of which Middle Congo was a part, to discuss the future of the French Empire in general and of the status of the African colonies in particular. Although all but one of the delegates were European, the spirit of the conference was very sympathetic to the rights of the African people. It was agreed that after the war the colonies would receive certain social and economic reforms, and assimilation would be made easier. Some powers formerly exercised in Paris would be transferred to the local African governments, forced labor would end, and African representation in the French parliament would be increased. The terms *union* and *overseas territories* would replace *empire* and *colonies,* and the people would be called *citizens* instead of *subjects.* Assemblies of African representatives would be established as local legislatures. But, just in case anyone was considering it, the possibility of independence for the colonies (whatever they were then to be called) was clearly rejected. "The aims of the civilizing work accomplished by France in the colonies exclude any thought of autonomy," the preamble to the conference's report stated. "The idea of establishing, even in the distant future, 'self-government' in the colonies must be discarded."

The new constitution of postwar France, approved in 1946, did in fact make all the promised concessions, but once the excitement of their improved status wore off, most Africans found they were not much better off than they had been. They were now citizens, but most of them did not have the educational and property requirements to vote, and while there were now territorial assemblies, all the real power remained in Paris, where African representation was small. Discontent with the status of "overseas territory" began to grow, and concerted nationalist sentiment began to emerge.

The only French political party that really sympathized with the problems and ambitions of the African territories was the Communist Party. In 1946 the French Communists sponsored a meeting in Bamako, the capital of the West African country then known as French Sudan (now Mali). Here African leaders from several territories formed an organization, the *Rassemblement Démocratique Africain* (African

*South African antiapartheid novelist Alan S. Paton, left, peers over his glasses as he exchanges comments with Léopold Sédar Senghor, president of Senegal, as they wait to receive honorary degrees from Harvard University, Cambridge, Massachusetts, 1971. (Courtesy AP/Wide World)*

Democratic Assembly, RDA), the first broad-based independence movement in French Africa. Of course the French government did what it could to suppress the RDA, and many leaders of African politics were afraid of associating with the Communist Party, which supported it. The delegates from French Sudan, Guinea, and Dahomey (now Benin), and the prestigious leader of Senegal, Léopold Senghor, refused to join.

Led by the wealthy coffee-planter and physician Félix Houphouët-Boigny of the Ivory Coast, the RDA was the only party with enough organization to make a sustained case for self-government, and it won many seats in the French National Assembly. It also inspired several other nationalist parties. In time, it stimulated enough ambition for independence to bring down France's overseas empire.

## MOROCCO AND TUNISIA (1956)

The breakup in French Africa began in the Arab north, where France's control had been modeled on Great Britain's policy of "indirect rule." In Morocco, France had governed through the local sultan. A postwar Muslim nationalist movement demanded independence in the name of its religious freedom, and the puppet government of Sultan Muhammed V supported the demand. France responded by exiling the sultan in 1953, but that only made matters worse. The popular monarch became a hero and the nationalist spirit grew, producing a Moroccan liberation army prepared to fight for the country's freedom. In Tunisia, the *Néo-Destour* (New Constitution) party (ND), which had agitated for national independence since the 1930s under the French-trained lawyer Habib Bourguiba, joined the movement, and France repeated its tactic by exiling its sovereign Munsif Bey. The result was the same; Tunisia's demands became more insistent, and all political parties joined the fight. Terrorism and sabotage wracked both countries as France continued to resist. Finally France capitulated. With a revolution already going on since 1954 in Algeria, France could not face another war, and in 1956 Morocco and Tunisia became the first French colonies in Africa to gain complete independence.

## FRENCH GUINEA (GUINEA, 1958)

After its defeat in North Africa, France reconsidered its colonial policy yet again. When de Gaulle assumed complete power in a new French

# SÉKOU TOURÉ (1922–84)

The first president of Guinea, Sékou Touré was a strong supporter of Pan-Africanism and the only African leader to reject France's offer of internal self-government as a part of the French "Community." His stubborn defiance was to cost his country years of isolation and confusion, but it stood as an inspiration to a continent seeking to end colonialism.

The son of a peasant farmer in French Guinea and a grandson of the 19th-century rebel leader Samori Touré, Sékou Touré studied at a technical school, where he was expelled for organizing a food strike at the age of 15. He took a job as a post-office clerk in the capital, Conakry, and formed a post and telegraph workers' union, Guinea's first trade union, at 23. Two years later, the dynamic young man helped form the Parti Démocratique de Guinée, which became a powerful nationalist movement. When the PDG won a majority of seats in the territorial assembly in 1957, the 35-year-old Touré became the colony's first prime minister.

When French president Charles de Gaulle demanded of the colonies a choice between complete independence, with no economic or military support, or membership in the federation he called the French Community, Touré refused the offer of help, calling it "the old merchandise with a new label," and said Guineans preferred poverty in freedom to riches in slavery. De Gaulle turned to his staff, said, "Well, gentlemen, there is a man we will never get on with," and left Guinea the next morning.

government in 1958, he sponsored a revised constitution that offered all France's remaining 12 colonies in West Africa a choice between full membership in a new federation called the French Community, a sort of French equivalent of the British Commonwealth, or total independence, which would mean the withdrawal of all French financial and technical support. It was a daring move.

While all the other colonies voted to stay with the French Community (the Ivory Coast vote was 99.9 percent for it), Guinea supported its popular leader by a 95 percent vote for independence and followed Ghana as the second country in tropical Africa to become free of colonial rule in 1958. France's revenge of diplomatic isolation, the withdrawal of health services, and the destruction of files and furniture, did not disrupt the country as much as de Gaulle hoped. Russia and Ghana were prompt to loan money. Touré became a hero among anticolonialists internationally and received a warm welcome at the United Nations. He continued to speak out against France's arrangement with the other former French colonies, and in 1960, a little more than a year after the Afro-French Community was established, its 13 members all demanded and received their complete independence.

Touré was immensely popular in his first years in office as a fearless champion of independence, but he came to fear that there was what he called "a permanent plot" to overthrow him. He became notorious for his suspicions, and an atmosphere of fear settled over the government. Police torture was common and more than 50 of his ministers of state and senior army officers were executed. Touré even blamed a cholera epidemic on his enemies' efforts to discredit him.

Touré's socialistic economic policies were equally destructive to his country. He imposed state control on all business and trade and made Guinea one of the poorest nations in Africa. Only in his last years did he begin to allow free trade. But although Sékou Touré was a harsh and often cruel dictator, he remains a heroic example of courageous anti-imperialism in the history of Africa.

De Gaulle was sure that French African politicians considered themselves more French than African, and that they realized how much their lands needed aid and cooperation from Paris. And he was proved almost completely right. All but one of the colonies chose to remain as self-governing states in the French Community. The only one to vote "no" was Guinea. "The people of Guinea prefer freedom in poverty to riches in slavery," its leader Sékou Touré told President de Gaulle.

The most radical of all French African politicians, Touré was the grandson of folk hero Samori Touré, who had fought to free Guinea from French rule in the 19th century, and his rejection of membership in the French Community was as defiant as his grandfather's had been.

*Sékou Touré, president of Guinea, around 1960.* (Courtesy Information Guinée)

France understood the insult clearly and made it equally clear what would happen to any other colony that was tempted to repeat it. Guinea received its independence abruptly within weeks, all aid was cut off at once, and Guineans in the army were dismissed without pensions. When the colonial administrators left the country, they ripped the telephones from the office walls, broke the windows, and smashed all the light fixtures. They even broke the dishes in the government dining room. Their final gesture was to destroy the prison records, so Guinean officials had to ask the prisoners what crimes they had committed and how long their sentences were.

## "THE YEAR OF AFRICA" 1960

Guinea was one of the French colonies least able to stand by itself, and France's harsh and vindictive treatment of it was a blow. Nevertheless, the new republic survived (partly by turning to the Soviet Union for aid, a response that angered France even further), and thus proved to other colonies that complete independence was possible. As political analyst Frantz Fanon observed, "The independence of a new territory, the liberation of a new people are felt by other oppressed countries as an invitation, an encouragement, and a promise."

With the examples of Ghana and Guinea, the idea of freedom swept the continent like a tropical storm. The French Community collapsed within a year as its members became disillusioned with French "assimilation." Between January and November 1960, "the Year of Africa," 15 French territories, including all of its West African colonies, demanded and received full independence, along with British Nigeria, the Belgian Congo (now Zaire), and Italian Somaliland, Italy's last holding on the continent. That year British prime minister Harold Macmillan ruefully summed up the situation on the continent in a famous speech to the white South African parliament:

> We have seen the awakening of national consciousness in peoples who have for centuries lived in dependence upon some other power. Fifteen years ago this movement spread through Asia. Today the same thing is happening in Africa. . . . The wind of change is blowing through the continent, and whether we like it

or not this growth of national consciousness is a political fact, and our national policies must take account of it.

The wind of change had been blowing—sometimes a gentle breeze and sometimes a fierce tempest—for a long time in Africa. In the French Empire, it had grown to gale velocity, and the rotten structure was toppling. Calling the colonies "overseas territories" wasn't enough, and neither was elevating them to members of the French Community. One by one they all pressed for full independence, and France was powerless to hold them.

## ALGERIA (1962)

With the disintegration of France's West and equatorial African holdings in 1960, only three territories remained to it on the continent. Of these, the most important was Algeria, the richest holding in the French Empire and the one it most bitterly resisted giving up.

The Arab territory of Algeria, along the Mediterranean coast of North Africa, had never existed as a nation before the French conquered the land between 1830 and 1847, but although it was formally annexed in 1834 and declared an integral part of France in 1848, Arab resistance remained strong for many years. By the 20th century, however, Algeria had been subdued, and its Arab majority asked no more than equality as citizens of France. The control by the white *colons*, the million or so French and other Europeans who owned the most productive lands and almost all of the mines and factories, was always racially discriminatory, excluding the 8 million Arabs from the best jobs and denying them social and educational advantages. After World War I, independence movements began to form, and by 1945 open conflict broke out between "the two nations" in Algeria. A revolt in the northeast, in which 100 *colons* were killed, resulted in the slaughter of 100,000 Arabs.

In 1947, France attempted to pacify the unhappy majority by extending full citizenship to the Muslims and establishing an elective Algerian assembly, but the efforts were not successful. In the assembly, representation of the two groups was equal although the Arabs outnumbered the *colons* by eight to one. The nationalists, most of whom had not demanded much more than modest social and political reforms until then, now demanded complete independence.

The movement was not organized into a revolutionary force, however, until 1954, when the *Front de Libération Nationale* (National Liberation Front, FLN) was founded. The FLN initiated a guerrilla war to force France out of Algeria and established a government-in-exile in Cairo in 1958. It was headed by Ferhat Abbas, a pioneer reformer who had fought for the freedom of his country for many years. Abbas had begun his work in the 1940s campaigning for a moderate assimilationist policy, but by the next decade had become a revolutionary. The war he led was one of the bloodiest in African colonial history.

French military superiority kept the revolution from succeeding for eight years, but at enormous cost in money and lives. By 1956 France was spending $2.8 million a day to crush the revolt and had more than half a million troops in Algeria. It had to surrender its claims to Morocco and Tunisia because it couldn't afford to fight on all three fronts. And the more concessions France offered in an effort to make peace, the worse things got. Free elections, internal rights, better schools and hospitals, equality as a part of the French Community—all these reforms angered the *colons* but failed to satisfy the FLN. At last, sickened by tales of atrocities committed on both sides and resigned to the impossibility of winning the war, the French capitulated. In 1962, after 132 years of French domination, Algeria became an independent republic. The colons, their advantages gone with the support of the government in Paris, left the country in droves.

Almost nothing remained of the French Empire in Africa after Algeria won its independence. The last survivor of French colonialism on the continent was French Somaliland, a small strip of land on the east coast where Somalia joins Ethiopia, valuable for its strategic position on the Red Sea and for its port. When the former British and Italian Somaliland became independent in 1960, nationalist parties formed in French Somaliland and began demonstrating for freedom. The Organization of African Unity, meeting in Ethiopia in 1963, added its support to their demand. France clung to this last shred of imperial power for a long time but finally, with a sigh, surrendered. In 1977 the French Empire in Africa came to an end when French Somaliland, renamed Djibouti for its capital city, became an independent nation.

## CHAPTER EIGHT NOTES

p. 90     "The colonial achievement in the Maghrib . . ." Jacques Berque. *French North Africa: The Maghrib Between the Two World Wars* (New York: Praeger, 1967), p. 93.

p. 91     "The aims of the civilizing work . . ." Preamble to the report of the Brazzaville Conference, 1944, quoted in Waldemar A. Nielsen. *The Great Powers and Africa* (New York: Praeger, 1969), p. 84.

p. 97     "The independence of a new territory . . ." Frantz Fanon. *Toward the African Revolution: Political Essays* (New York: Grove Press, 1967), p. 145.

pp. 97–98 "We have seen the awakening of national consciousness . . ." Harold Macmillan, speech delivered in Cape Town, South Africa, 1960, quoted in Roland Oliver and Anthony Atmore. *Africa Since 1800* (Cambridge, England: Cambridge University Press, 1981), p. 273.

# INDEPENDENCE FOR THE BELGIAN COLONIES

The Republic of the Congo has been proclaimed, and our land is now in the hands of her own children. . . .

>—Patrice Lumumba, first prime minister of the Republic of the Congo (now Zaire), in his Independence Day address, June 30, 1960

If Great Britain's plan for its colonies was eventual independence, and France's was assimilation, Belgium seems to have been without any long-term plan except to keep things the same. Once King Léopold was forced to relinquish his personal ownership of the Congo territory to the Belgian government in 1908, the colony became a model of efficiency and humanity. The living standards of the Congolese were not only higher than they had been before the Belgians came, they were higher than those of any other native population in Africa. Belgium thought that such generosity—the good schools, hospitals, roads, and jobs it provided—would be enough to keep "their"

# PATRICE LUMUMBA (1925–61)

Few African statesmen came from less promising backgrounds than Patrice Lumumba, the first premier of the Republic of the Congo (now Zaire) and revered by many as a martyr for the cause of African political independence.

Lumumba was born in a tribal society in the Belgian Congo and attended mission schools. He finished high school, although he was dismissed from one because he argued with his teachers, and at the age of 19 he took a job as a post office clerk. At 30 he was convicted of embezzling postal funds and sentenced to a year in prison. Upon his release he worked as a salesman for a beer company.

Active since his post office days in nationalist groups, Lumumba helped organize the *Mouvement National Congolais* (MNC), a party standing for political independence and strong central government, and in 1958 he became its president by simply typing his name with that title on a list of the party's officers and releasing it to the newspapers. When other party leaders protested and attempted to expel him, the MNC split into two factions, and Lumumba's wing became the stronger.

A passionate spokesman for national self-government, Lumumba was jailed by the Belgian authorities in 1959 for

Africans happy. It also thought that it could keep them so isolated that they would never catch independence fever.

## THE BELGIAN CONGO (ZAIRE, 1960)

Of course they were wrong. Despite their relatively good treatment and the prosperity of the colony, the people of the Belgian Congo began to think of national independence as early as those of any territory on the continent. The only difference between Congolese anticolonialism and that of the native peoples of British and French Africa was that the subjects of the strict, "paternal" Belgian colony had almost no available outlet for public protest. As early as 1921, Simon Kimbangu's religious making a speech that called for "a positive plan for the immediate liberation of the Congo" and nonviolent resistance to colonial rule. When the colony was liberated in 1960, Lumumba was elected prime minister and shocked many at the independence day ceremony by denouncing Belgian colonial rule.

Although enthusiastically supported by his followers, Lumumba had an equally vigorous opposition. Many Congolese wanted the new country to be a federation of tribal states rather than a unified nation with the main power in the hands of the national government. Lumumba's chief rival in the 1960 election was Joseph Kasavubu, president of another political party. The election had been so close that Kasavubu was given the honorary position of president. Within days of the proclamation of independence, army mutinies and tribal secessions tore the country apart, and Lumumba and Kasavubu tried to dismiss each other from office. Lumumba declared martial law and called on the United Nations to restore peace, but he was forced from office by the military and arrested.

Sent to Katanga province, a stronghold of his enemies and one of the regions that had tried to secede from the union, he was murdered in January 1961. His tragic death at the age of 35 made him a symbol of national unity for the country that he helped lead to freedom.

movement had begun indirectly stirring up rebellion, and as the desire for independence increased in the 1950s it became an active force, establishing links with Afro-Christian churches and with opponents of colonialism throughout West and Central Africa. If protest did not appear openly for so long, it was because the Belgians kept a tight lid on it.

The first substantial call for change came from outside the continent. In 1955 a professor of colonial legislation at Antwerp University in Belgium, A. A. J. van Bilsen, published a pamphlet entitled *A Thirty-Year Plan for the Political Emancipation of Belgian Africa*. It was a cautious proposal, but the Belgians considered it dangerously revolu-

*Premier Patrice Lumumba, right, stands with president Joseph Kasavubu (wearing a Lokele chief's hat) at the airport in Léopoldville (now Kinshasa), 1960.* (Courtesy AP/Wide World)

tionary—and they were right. It was the first time the word *emancipation* had appeared in print with reference to the Congo, and it echoed loudly among the small group of radicals in the colony. The next year *Conscience Africaine*, a Catholic journal published in the Congolese capital, Léopoldville, carried a "Manifesto" applauding van Bilsen's suggestion and urging its acceptance. The idea, long suppressed, had finally surfaced.

Among the earliest outlets for dissent were the cultural societies that had sprung up in the early 1950s to support and sustain tribal traditions.

One such organization, the *Alliance des Ba-Kongo* (ABAKO), turned itself into a decisive political party among the Kongo people in 1956 when local elections were held in Léopoldville. ABAKO took a very clear stand on the issue of national independence in a statement challenging the *Conscience Africaine* manifesto for being too moderate. Thirty years was too long for ABAKO. "Our patience is already exhausted," it urged. "Emancipation should be granted us this very day." The call struck a responsive chord, and ABAKO swept the field in the Léopoldville elections under the leadership of Joseph Kasavubu, a schoolteacher who had studied for the priesthood before going into politics.

Another tribal society that became a political force in the drive for independence came from the copper-rich province of Katanga. The Lunda Tribal Association, which in 1959 changed its name to the *Confédération des Associations Tribales du Katanga* (CONAKAT), also began as a cultural organization dedicated to preserving ethnic interests, but under the leadership of businessman Moïse Tschombe became a powerful political force.

Two events outside the country in 1958 spurred the Congolese anticolonial movement to action. The first was de Gaulle's offer of independence to the French Congo. Two days after de Gaulle's announcement, a group of political activists in the Belgian Congo sent the Belgian colonial minister a petition calling for independence. The demand was rejected, but within weeks the group created the first nationwide political party in the country, the *Mouvement National Congolais* (MNC). Its president, Patrice Lumumba, was neither a teacher nor a businessman but an ex-postal clerk with no more than an elementary-school education who, until shortly before, had been much more modest in his political expectations. In 1956 he had written a petition to the Belgian government asking for nothing more than "rather more liberal measures" within the colonial framework for the small Congolese elite.

The second event took place in the newly independent republic of Ghana, where Kwame Nkrumah had organized a Pan-African meeting. Reflecting the spirit of the Pan-African Conference he had attended in London in 1900, where he had come under the influence of W. E. B. Du Bois, Nkrumah was seeking to promote unity among the nations of the continent. The All-African People's Conference, held in Ghana's

# LUMUMBA'S INDEPENDENCE DAY ADDRESS

Men and women of the Congo, who have fought for and won the Independence we celebrate today, I salute you in the name of the Congolese government. . . .

No Congolese worthy of the name will ever be able to forget that that independence has only been won by struggle, a struggle that went on day after day, a struggle of fire and idealism, a struggle in which we have spared neither effort, deprivation, suffering, or even our blood.

This struggle, involving tears, fire and blood, is something of which we are proud in our deepest hearts, for it was a noble and just struggle, which was needed to bring to an end the humiliating slavery imposed upon us by force. . . .

We have experienced contempt, insults and blows, morning, noon and night, because we were "blacks." . . .

We have seen our lands despoiled in the name of so-called legal documents which were no more than a recognition of superior force.

We have seen the appalling suffering of those who had their political opinions and religious beliefs dismissed; as exiles in their own country their lot was truly worse than death.

capital, Accra, included political leaders from 28 African countries, including many not yet independent, and its spirit was truly international. It called on the world's super-powers to discontinue the testing of atomic weapons and urged African nations to adopt a unified foreign policy "to further the cause of peace." Above all, it demanded that "a definite date be set for the attainment of independence by each of the colonial territories." Such demands may have had little effect on the colonial powers, who for the most part ignored the Accra conference, but the effect on the still-uncertain independence movements in Africa was electric. Kwame Nkrumah, as the president of the first country to gain its freedom in "Black Africa," was a popular hero whose voice carried great weight.

> We have seen magnificent houses in the towns for the whites, and crumbling straw huts for the blacks. . . .
>
> We have known that the law was never the same for a white man as it was for a black: for the former it made allowances, for the latter it was cruel and inhuman. . . .
>
> All this has meant the most profound suffering.
>
> But all this, we can now say . . . we who have suffered in body and mind from colonialist oppression, all this is now ended.
>
> The Republic of the Congo has been proclaimed, and our land is now in the hands of her own children. . . .
>
> The liberation of the Congo marks a decisive step towards the liberation of the whole African continent. . . .
>
> Long live the independence and unity of Africa!
>
> Long live the sovereign and independent Congo!
>
> —Patrice Lumumba, address at the ceremony marking the independence of the Republic of the Congo (now Zaire), June 30, 1960.

Kasavubu, who had been invited to the conference, had been unable to attend because he lacked the necessary vaccination to travel, but Lumumba went and was inspired. He returned to address a mass rally in Léopoldville with a passionate message of Pan-African unity in the struggle against imperialism. "Independence is not a gift," he told the crowd, "but a fundamental right of the Congo." Soon the capital was the scene of violent rioting.

By 1959 rival organizations such as BALUBAKAT, a Katanga-based group dedicated to the interests of the Baluba tribe, emerged to make their own demands. New political ambitions and old tribal and regional hostilities flared into violence throughout the country. There were clashes between rival parties. Kasavubu's ABAKO wanted to maintain tribal identities and favored a loose federation of states. Tschombe wanted Katanga to become a separate country. Lumumba and his MNC favored a unified nation with a strong central government. Racial tensions also increased, and there were attacks on white settlers and even missionary churches. The Belgian police and military troops were unable to maintain order. Both Lumumba and Kasavubu were arrested, but their popularity was too great for the government to keep them in prison more than a few months. It was clear, even to the Belgians, that something would have to be done if another Algerian-type war was to be avoided.

A quick series of political concessions and constitutional reforms followed in an effort at calming the troubled waters, but there was no turning back the tide. In 1960, Belgium recognized that its best hope for salvaging anything of its economic holdings in the territory was to grant independence, and it surrendered. Deeply divided among themselves, the Congo's many parties hammered together a new government with Patrice Lumumba as prime minister and his rival Joseph Kasavubu as president in an uneasy alliance that did not last long. The Democratic Republic of the Congo was officially declared independent on June 30, 1960, and renamed Zaire in 1971.

## RUANDA (RWANDA) AND URUNDI (BURUNDI) (1962)

The two small mountainous territories of Ruanda and Urundi adjoining the Belgian Congo on its eastern border were part of Germany's Tanganyika colony from 1899 till 1916, when they were seized by Congolese troops, and administered as a portion of the Congo colony when the League of Nations assigned them to Belgium in 1919. However, they did not share in the Congo's independence in 1960 because of their peculiar racial situation.

The ethnic composition of these two ancient tribal kingdoms is the same. The shorter, darker-skinned Bahutu, constituting over 85 percent of the population, live as peasant farmers, while the tall, slim Batutsi, averaging over six-foot-six in height, are the politically dominant tribe and the traditional rulers. Hoping to preserve their control of the Bahutu, the aristocratic Batutsi supported the independence movement during the 1950s, but the Belgians rejected their demand, following the British example in Southern Rhodesia by refusing to grant independence unless the colonies had majority rule.

The Bahutu in Ruanda formed a political party, the *Parti d'Emancipation des Hutus* (PARMEHUTU). There was widespread violence, especially in Ruanda, as the Bahutu turned against their oppressors with a ferocity born of centuries of bitterness. Many of the Batutsi fled to Urundi, where the two races lived with somewhat less conflict. The differences between the two regions made it obvious that they could not be granted independence as one state, and in 1961 Belgium arranged a vote in Ruanda in which the majority agreed to end the Batutsi monarchy. In July 1962, the two became independent, Ruanda as a republic and Urundi as a constitutional monarchy, and both resumed the traditional African spellings of their names.

## CHAPTER NINE NOTES

p. 101    "The Republic of the Congo has been proclaimed . . ." Patrice Lumumba, in his address on June 30, 1960, marking the independence of the Republic of the Congo (now Zaire).

p. 105    "Our patience is already exhausted . . ." Quoted in René Lemarchand. *Political Awakening in the Belgian Congo* (Berkeley, Calif.: University of California Press, 1964), p. 157.

pp. 106– "Men and women of the Congo . . ." Patrice Lumumba, in his
107    address marking independence of the Republic of the Congo (now Zaire), June 30, 1960, quoted in Thomas Kanza. *The Rise and Fall of Patrice Lumumba: Conflict in the Congo* (Boston, Mass.: G.K. Hall, 1979), pp. 161–64.

p. 106    ". . . a definite date be set . . ." The First Conference of Independent African States, Accra, April, 1958. Quoted in Colin Legum. *Pan-Africanism* (New York: Praeger, 1962), pp. 139–48.

p. 107    "Independence is not a gift . . ." Quoted in Lemarchand, p. 161.

# INDEPENDENCE FOR THE SPANISH AND PORTUGUESE COLONIES

The guerrilla manuals once told us that without mountains you cannot make guerrilla war. But in my country there are no mountains, only the people. The people are our mountains.
—Amilcar Cabral, leader of the African Party for the Independence of Guinea and Cape Verde

The Spanish and the Portuguese, like the Belgians, were unprepared for the spread of African nationalism because they had never accepted the possibility of national independence for their colonies. Spain was neither deeply invested in Africa nor prepared to defend its colonial possessions, so its response was a calculated withdrawal of authority where necessary and an effort at maintaining a foothold where possible. The Portuguese response was more determined, and the result was one of the bloodiest wars of liberation on the continent.

## SPANISH AFRICA

Spain's colonial experience in Africa was a brief and inglorious one. Concerned almost exclusively with commercial exploitation and indifferent to the welfare of the peoples whose land and labor it took, the Spanish were deaf to protest and ruthless in its suppression. They encountered almost continuous opposition wherever they tried to establish themselves. The fierce Arabs of North Africa and the resolute Fang tribe of Guinea and the nearby islands off the west coast were uniform in their refusal to submit, and although superior Spanish arms and manpower eventually prevailed, the business of colonizing Africa finally proved too costly to support.

### Morocco (1956)

The slice of northern Morocco that France left to Spain when it occupied the area in 1912 was small, poor, and hard to defend. Its mountainous terrain and the fierce independence of its people made it a trouble spot for the Spanish. Although national pride and the dream of finding a way to make the land pay kept them there for 54 years, the Spanish were under constant attack from various Arab chieftains and never reaped any reward for their determination.

In 1921 the opposition to Spanish rule in Morocco intensified when the first large-scale nationalist resistance began, and Spain suffered the worst European defeat in African history. In that year the Spanish broke an agreement with the Berbers of the Rif mountains and invaded Xauen, the Muslim holy city of the Rifs. The Rif chieftain Abd el-Krim, a former judge and a brilliant military leader, launched a rebellion against Spanish rule that shattered the European army. In the battle of Anual in 1921, the Spanish lost between 13,000 and 19,000 lives and were forced to withdraw. The Rif troops pursued, and by 1922 they occupied enough territory to proclaim an independent Islamic republic. It was not until Abd el-Krim crossed the border into French Morocco to continue his conquest that the combined armies of the two countries succeeded in capturing him in 1926. Even then he was able to escape, at the age of 65, and lived out the rest of his days in Cairo, organizing rebel forces to liberate Morocco.

Although Abd el-Krim was finally defeated, the skilled desert warrior became a popular hero and an inspiration to nationalist organizers in both Spanish and French Morocco. When the French surrendered their Moroccan territory under the pressure of the Algerian revolt in 1956, the Spanish gave up their own troublesome and unprofitable holdings there without much protest.

### Spanish Guinea (Equatorial Guinea, 1968)
The Spanish had had conflicts with the Fang tribe of Río Muñi, the mainland region of Equatorial Guinea, since the European plantation owners began to develop the colony's cocoa industry in 1875. When the nationalist fever took hold in West Africa in the 1950s, the Fang became a unified voice opposing the inclusion of the region as part of Spain. Following the pattern of England, France, and Belgium, Spain granted Equatorial Guinea some token reforms, but the most powerful independence movement in the country, the Fang-based *Movimiento Nacional de Liberación de Guinea Ecuatorial* (MONALIGE) pressed for complete independence. The Spanish were unable to withstand the unceasing attacks of the Fang, and in 1968 they unhappily gave up their only remaining territory in "Black Africa."

### Spanish Sahara (Western Sahara)
The Spanish occupation of Spanish Sahara met with open revolt from the beginning. The native Sahrawi people had lived at peace with the French, but Spanish exploitation in the 1960s and 1970s generated widespread nationalist feeling. Spontaneous and disorganized, the protests of the Arab people were quickly and easily suppressed by the Spanish until 1973, when a group of students founded the *Frente Popular para la Liberación de Sekia el Hamra y Río de Oro* (POLISARIO) and launched a series of guerrilla attacks that continue today. In a Pan-African spirit of nationalist solidarity, as well as from loyalty to their fellow Muslims, the people of Algeria and Libya came to the aid of POLISARIO, providing them with arms and money. The desert fighters of the Sahara are skilled at combat and unyielding in their demands for the independence of the two provinces of Spanish Sahara,

*Supporters of POLISARIO demonstrating at Ausred, Spanish Sahara, 1975.* (Courtesy United Nations 130170 Y. Nagata)

Sakiet el Hamra and Río de Oro. In 1976 POLISARIO proclaimed itself a sovereign nation with dominion over the sparsely settled region, and demanded recognition as the Sahrawi (Sahara) Arab Democratic Republic (SADR).

Spain realized that it could not stand up to POLISARIO and quickly withdrew in 1974, but both Morocco and Mauritania claimed the territory. The three governments have yet to agree. The OAU and 67 independent countries have so far recognized the SADR—and POLISARIO as its government—but Morocco and Mauritania divided the region up between themselves in 1976 and refuse to relinquish their claims. The fighting has gone on, costing Morocco over $100 million a year. The United Nations had scheduled a vote in 1992 to decide whether Western Sahara would become an independent country or be absorbed by Morocco, but the meeting never took place.

## PORTUGUESE AFRICA

Portugal was the first European country to establish a colonial empire in Africa, and except for some small, isolated territories like the French Djibouti or the British Seychelle Islands, it was one of the last to leave.

# CABRAL ON THE SITUATION IN PORTUGUESE GUINEA

*Amilcar Cabral, PAIGC secretary-general, at a meeting of the Special Meeting on Decolonization, Conakry, Guinea, 1972.* (Courtesy United Nations Y. Nagata/ARA)

We are not only underdeveloped, but not developed at all. The situation in my country, before the struggle, was that agriculture was the main basis of our economy. About 60 percent of the exportation in the country were peanuts. We didn't have any kind of industry. Only 14 persons had passed the university until 1960 . . . 99.7 percent . . . were illiterate. We had only two hospitals . . . only 300 beds for the sick people. The mortality for children in some regions was about 80 percent. You can realize what kind of a situation we had after . . . more than 500 years of Portuguese presence in our country.

—Amilcar Cabral, address to the U.S. House Committee on Foreign Affairs, Subcommittee on Africa, February 26, 1970

While all the rest of the continent was achieving nationhood, through the heady "Year of Africa," it refused even to discuss the idea of independence, insisting that all its colonies were "overseas provinces" of Portugal. These colonies had a psychological value as remnants of a once-great empire to a country that had become small and weak. They had economic value too: Angola and Mozambique were a valuable source of raw material and an important market for Portugal.

Portugal probably had the worst reputation in Europe for its treatment of its colonies—at least, after Léopold had been forced to sell his Congo to the Belgian government. The explorer David Livingstone had written of his visit to Portuguese East Africa, "Not a single native has been taught to read, not one branch of trade has been developed, and wherever Portuguese power . . . extends, we have that [slave] traffic in full force; which may be said to reverse every law of Christ and to defy the vengeance of heaven." It was to take more than a century, but Portugal's treatment of its subjects was finally to face the vengeance of man as well.

### Portuguese Guinea (Guinea-Bissau, 1974)

Despite its repressive government, Portugal was not able to keep educated Africans from noticing what was happening all over the continent, and by the 1950s groups were forming to challenge their colonial status. One of the first was the *Partido Africano da Independência de Guiné e Cabo Verde* (PAIGC), founded by an agricultural engineer named Amilcar Cabral in 1956. In 1959, PAIGC organized a peaceful strike of dockworkers in the port of Bissau, the capital, for higher wages. The Portuguese responded with exceptional brutality, and the massacre that followed sparked a full-scale war in 1963. The bloody conflict finally brought independence to Portuguese Guinea in 1974 and the Cape Verde islands off its coast in 1975. Portuguese Guinea was renamed Guinea-Bissau, from its capital city, to distinguish it from the former French colony, now called simply Guinea.

### Angola (1975)

The revolution in Angola began earlier and lasted longer than Cabral's in Guinea-Bissau. Some say it began in the 16th century because there had hardly been a year since then when there was not an anti-Portuguese campaign in this rich territory. The final one, which ended Portugal's presence there, began in 1961, when the *Movimento Popular de Libertação de Angola* (MPLA), the principal independence movement in the colony, organized an attack on the police headquarters

# AMILCAR CABRAL
## (1924 – 1973)

Described as "the inspired genius of the liberation movement in Portuguese Guinea," the revolutionary leader Amilcar Cabral was the founder of the African Party for the Independence of Guinea and Cape Verde (PAIGC), the most successful and advanced of all the freedom organizations in Africa in the 1960s and early 1970s.

Cabral was the son of an official and landowner in the Portuguese colony of Cape Verde. He went to school on that island and was such an outstanding student he received a scholarship to study agronomy and hydraulics engineering in Portugal. After he graduated in 1953, he went to Portuguese Guinea, where he was one of four university graduates in the country and had no trouble getting a good job as a government agricultural engineer. In his work, which took him throughout the country making surveys, he saw the oppression of the farmers there. He decided that political organization was necessary and began to meet with others to discuss ways of persuading the government to make reforms. "We didn't think about independence," he said later. "We hoped at that moment to . . . have civil rights, to be men, not treated like animals. . . . We received as answer only repression, imprisonment, torture."

Cabral remained a moderate and formed PAIGC in 1956 to protest against the economic and social conditions of his country. But the Portuguese were deaf to the party's complaints. In 1959 PAIGC organized a peaceful strike of dockworkers in the port of Bissau, the capital, for higher wages. The government responded with characteristic brutality, gunning down 50

in Luanda, the capital, to release some political prisoners and protest forced labor. Portuguese police and vigilantes responded by indiscriminately killing hundreds of Africans, including women and children, throughout the city. This, in turn, brought on uprisings elsewhere in the country, and inspired numerous other nationalist groups throughout the colony.

unarmed workers. This changed Cabral from a patient reformer to a revolutionary.

Moving the headquarters of PAIGC to Conakry, the capital of the newly independent Republic of Guinea (formerly a French colony), he initiated a full-scale war of liberation. He organized a guerrilla-training program and built an efficient and dedicated army. One major battle against the Portuguese was on the island of Como, an important PAIGC base, where 3,000 Portuguese soldiers battled some 300 of Cabral's troops for 75 days without success. The PAIGC victory was an important psychological victory for the independence movement.

The PAIGC forces under Cabral had widespread support, not only in Portuguese Guinea and Cape Verde, but internationally. By 1971 the desperate band of a few hundred guerrillas had grown to a disciplined army of over 8,000 soldiers, trained and equipped at first in the neighboring Republic of Guinea by Soviet and Algerian sympathizers. And by 1971, the 80 Portuguese garrisons that fought them had dwindled to 35, and more than half of Portuguese Guinea was under PAIGC control. In 1974, the heroic independence movement organized by Cabral forced Portugal to grant the colony independence.

A man of wide vision as well as great military skill, Cabral stressed education, health, and women's rights and was able to achieve national unity despite the long-standing ethnic conflicts within his country. Unfortunately, he did not live to see his success. He was assassinated in 1973, a year before the dream for which he lived came true. Years later, Tanzanian president Julius Nyerere said of Cabral, "He may have been the greatest leader of all Africa."

The MPLA was started as an underground nationalist movement by Agostinho Neto, later the first president of an independent Angola. The son of a Methodist minister and one of the few Angolans to complete a secondary education in those days, he went on to study medicine in Portugal and returned as a physician and a respected poet. Under Neto's command, the MPLA was to conduct the longest colonial war

*The end of Portuguese rule in Angola: Dr. Agostinho Neto speaking in the capital, Luanda, at the flag-raising ceremony, independence day, November 11, 1975.* (Courtesy United Nations 131272 J. P. Laffont)

in Africa's history, ending only with Portugal's defeat—and the independence of Angola—in 1975.

## Mozambique (1975)

In 1964, yet another colonial war broke out, this time in the large East African colony of Mozambique. The *Frente de Libertação de Moçambique* (FRELIMO), founded two years before by Eduardo Mondlane, launched an attack on the Portuguese that brought the army to its knees and contributed to the fall of the Portuguese government in Lisbon. Mondlane, the founder of modern Mozambique nationalism, brought an unusually international perspective to the independence movement. He had studied in South Africa, Portugal, and the United States, where he received a Ph.D. in sociology and anthropology at Northwestern University and went on to become an officer of the United Nations Trusteeship Council and teach at Syracuse University in New York. A close friend of both Cabral and Neto, Mondlane was a powerful force for unity in the deeply divided nationalist movement in Portuguese Africa until he was assassinated in 1969.

The Mozambique war of liberation was the final straw for Portugal. Four colonial wars at the same time were a luxury for which it had neither the money nor the manpower. The defense of its hopeless position in Africa was consuming nearly half of Portugal's annual budget by the 1960s, and it had cost the Portuguese the sympathy and support of every other country in the world except for South Africa. So although it was humiliating to surrender to people they considered uncivilized, the first of the colonial powers in Africa gave up the last of its empire in 1975. Angola and Mozambique, and the two island groups, Cape Verde and Saõ Tomé and Príncipe, were all declared free, independent nations. Like all new countries, they had some hard times ahead of them, but a new day was at last dawning in Africa.

## CHAPTER 10 NOTES

p. 110    "The guerrilla manuals once told us . . ." Amilcar Cabral, quoted in George M. Houser. *No One Can Stop the Rain* (New York: The Pilgrim Press, 1989), p. 199.

p. 114    "We are not only underdeveloped, . . ." Amilcar Cabral, 1970, quoted in Houser, p. 201.

p. 115    "Not a single native has been taught to read . . ." Charles and David Livingstone. *Narrative of an Expedition to the Zambezi and Its Tributaries*, 1866, quoted in James Duffy. *Portuguese Africa* (Harmondsworth, England: Penguin, 1962), p. 16.

# INDEPENDENCE
# AND AFTER

Civilized or not civilized, ignorant or illiterate, rich or poor,
we the African states deserve a government of our own
choice. Let us make our own mistakes, but let us take
comfort that they are our own mistakes.
> —Tom Mboya of Kenya, speech at the All
> African People's Conference (AAPC), 1958

The road to freedom for Africa has been a long and
steep one. Social, political, religious, and military resistance occurred
in all parts of the continent from the first days of European conquest.
It took many forms, from politely worded pleas for reform, through
work-strikes, boycotts, and public demonstrations, to full-scale war.
But for many years opposition to colonialism met with little success.
African independence movements were powerless before European
military might, and by the beginning of World War II, organized
large-scale conflict had virtually ended, except in the Belgian Congo
and the Portuguese colonies, where African resistance never ceased.
Elsewhere on the continent, most open struggle was replaced by efforts
at improving conditions through negotiation.

But in the 1940s several factors combined to renew the Africans' efforts to reclaim their own lands. First of all, the European mobilization of an African labor and military force during World War II gave the peoples of the continent a sense of their own place in the world and a realization of their potential. The increased education and exposure to the rest of the world that they received in the war made it clear that they had both the right and the power to seize their freedom, and by then their years of fruitless opposition had demonstrated that seizing it was the only way they were going to get it. They had the example of India, Burma, and Ceylon, newly freed from British rule, to support their hopes. The ringing words of the Atlantic Charter in 1941 and the United Nations Charter in 1945 demonstrated international sympathy for their cause. The tide of history had begun to turn against imperialism everywhere. Two non-European powers, the United States and the Soviet Union, dominated the world, and both were profoundly opposed to colonialism. A new age of liberty was coming. 〉

The spread of nationalism in Africa after World War II was different from that of Asia, emerging at the same time, because most of the African colonies had not been nations before the Europeans came. The boundary lines drawn on maps in Europe at the partition of the continent had little to do with the ancient kingdoms or tribal territories of the people living there. So it was not a sense of loyalty to their countries, artificially created and defined for them by the Europeans, that inspired African resistance. Rather it was a hatred of colonialism and a determination to be free of foreign control.

Freedom came with surprising speed, once it began, for most of the continent. One by one the independence movements drove home their demands, and one by one the European colonial powers accepted defeat. In the 20 years following the liberation of the Gold Coast in 1957, some 44 European colonies in Africa won their freedom. In 1960 alone, 17 new nations were created. The Europeans, seeing the handwriting on the wall, scrambled out of the continent as fast as they had scrambled in. Sometimes the final negotiations and new constitutions were finished just days before the official dates of independence. The surrender of mineral rights to the Africans in Northern Rhodesia was still being worked out at a garden party on the lawn of Government House a few hours before the ceremony that made that colony independent as Zambia in 1964.

# THE ORGANIZATION OF
## AFRICAN UNITY

Since long before the first of the European colonies in Africa achieved its independence, the dream had been alive of an Africa free and united. African-Americans and West Indians wrote of African unity in the 19th century, and it was one of the goals expressed at the Pan-African Conference in London in 1900. But it was not until new nations began to emerge from colonialism on the continent that the idea began to take shape.

Seventeen African nations gained their freedom in 1960, two more the next year, and four in 1962. By 1963, there were 32 independent countries on the continent, and a need was felt for a multinational group to regulate issues among them, protect their international rights, and work to bring about the freedom of the 20 remaining colonies in Africa. The first meeting of the Organization of African Unity (OAU) was called in May 1963 by Emperor Haile Selassie of Ethiopia, the oldest independent state on the continent, in his capital, Addis Ababa.

Now made up of 50 members, the OAU includes every independent nation on the continent except two. South Africa has been rejected because of its policy of racial discrimination, and Morocco refuses to join because the organization recognizes the independence of Western Sahara, which Morocco claims as its own territory.

In the 30 years since the OAU began, it has had several impressive successes. Dedicated to respecting the boundaries established for each of its members at independence, it has played an important role in holding countries together.

The removal of European government, which the colonists preferred to call by the polite term "transfer of power," was not always a friendly process. Although few colonial governments ripped out the telephones and destroyed the files when they left, as the French did in Guinea, many were driven out by force and fought their expulsion bitterly. Especially in the colonies that had large Euro-

It is credited with putting an end to the civil war in Sudan in 1973 by mediation, it has helped bring international pressure to bear on South Africa's racial discrimination, and it has established continent-wide economic policies to assure mutual cooperation on financial matters and is working toward the goal of a single, unified African economy.

The OAU has had its share of failures too. Because it has no military force, it has been unable to do anything during the civil wars in Nigeria and Angola or to curb the brutality of dictators. Because the head of state of every member country has an automatic turn as president of the OAU, the organization has been led by some very controversial figures, and this has sometimes cost it international prestige. There have been conflicts between various blocs of nations, which have prevented the Organization of African Unity from acting with complete unity itself. Also, the OAU has consistently suffered from financial problems, since many of its members have been unable to pay their dues.

But although the OAU has not always been able to accomplish its goals effectively, it remains the voice of Africa in the United Nations and in the rest of the world, and its prestige remains high. Still headquartered in Addis Ababa, it has established special committees on economy, education, health, defense, and science that have helped to draw the countries together on major programs. These programs include the development of cooperative medical facilities, joint industrial projects, international roads and telephone lines, and standardization of schools. Conflicts still exist among the many new nations in Africa, but the OAU offers hope that the continent is progressing toward the old dream of a united Africa.

pean populations, freedom was handed over reluctantly and often with bad feelings on both sides. When Patrice Lumumba took office as the prime minister of the Belgian Congo (now Zaire) in 1960, the king of Belgium insulted the Africans at the ceremony, and Lumumba replied with an angry speech recalling the oppression his country had endured.

# CONTEMPORARY
# AFRICAN FICTION

The fiction written in and about Africa when the continent was first colonized was generally limited to adventure stories about white hunters and explorers, and the writers naturally tended to imitate the literature of the countries controlling each territory. British colonists, and Africans in British colonies, wrote like the writers in Great Britain, and those from French-speaking colonies imitated France. In time, however, a modern literature reflecting African culture began to emerge. Naturally this literature is as diverse as the peoples of Africa themselves, but much of it shares the sense of protest, the social commitment, and the ethnic pride of the emerging nations that have produced it.

Protest against colonialism and a yearning for independence has often been subtly expressed or concealed with humor in books coming from the new African countries. Amos Tutuola disguises his anger as fantasy from his Yoruba background in such novels as *The Palm-Wine Drinkard*, which reveal the pain of the African in amusing dialect. Chinua Achebe mixes humor and sadness in his novels. In *Things Fall Apart*, published in 1958, he describes the collision of cultures when the Europeans came to his native Nigeria, and in *A Man of the People* (1966) he makes bitter fun of the emerging African middle-class. Wole Soyinka, a Nobel prize–winning poet, playwright, and novelist, also presents a contrast between the Nigeria of his youth and the Europeanized nation it became. In *The Interpreters* (1967) he paints an ironic picture of Africans who try to imitate the British they despise.

The conflict between the old and the new is not the only subject of protest literature in contemporary Africa. Racial

Different European countries saw the transition differently. Belgium, Portugal, and Spain viewed it as a surrender to victorious enemies, but Great Britain recognized the change as inevitable and accepted it with resignation, incorporating its former colonies into its Commonwealth as full and equal partners. "We did not 'lose' an discrimination in white-ruled South Africa has long been an important theme for fiction, much of it coming from sympathetic white authors. Perhaps the South African novelist best known internationally is Alan Paton, whose 1948 *Cry, the Beloved Country*, a simple story of a black man destroyed by the white society, is a classic fictional attack on the racist policies of his government. Dan Jacobson's touching *A Dance in the Sun* (1956) demonstrates the mutual dependency of a black servant and a white master. The popular white playwright Athol Fugard has written many plays dramatizing the clash of races in South Africa. Such dramas as *The Blood Knot* (1968) have been presented all over the world. The white South African writer Nadine Gordimer received the Nobel Prize in 1991 for her sensitive and complex novels revealing how racism in her country dehumanizes the white society that imposes it.

As the newly independent countries of Africa have learned to cope with their own internal problems, writers of fiction have found other subjects besides colonial rule and racism. Ghanaian novelist Ayi Kwei Armah, for example, has written powerfully about corrupt post-independence politics in such novels as *The Beautyful Ones Are Not Yet Born* (1966), in which he reports that since the whites left office there has been no improvement in government, only "a change of embezzlers and a change of the hunters and the hunted." Among the most important writers of recent years, Kenya's Ngugi wa Thiong'o reveals the cultural changes in his country's society by focusing on the life of a small rural village.

In the short time since Africa struck off the bonds of white rule, it has begun to find its own voice in literature. As a new generation of writers has come to terms with the complex situation of the continent, a new and eloquent fiction has emerged to express it.

Empire," one British cabinet member wrote in 1965. "We followed to its logical end what has always been British colonial policy." France too tried to maintain as much connection as its former African colonies permitted. Its official position—at least, initially—was that, except for Guinea, the new countries that had been its colonies became French "overseas territories" and were therefore still a part of France. However unwillingly these colonial governments had handed over their power, they tried to establish mutually profitable trade and diplomatic alliances.

Although bad feelings persisted in the former Belgian and Portuguese colonies and in such cases as Guinea, the actual conclusion of the struggle for independence was usually peaceful, with both sides sitting as friends across the conference table willing to cooperate in peace. When Jomo Kenyatta was elected prime minister of Kenya, after

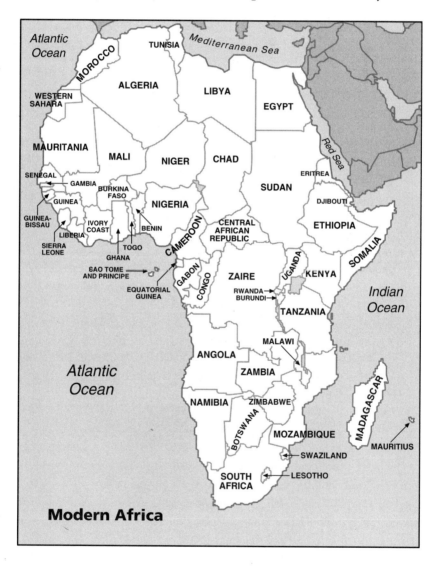

**Modern Africa**

nine years of cruel imprisonment, he urged the British settlers to remain in Africa, calling on whites and blacks to join hands and work together for the benefit of the country.

But even where the "transfer of power" was relatively smooth, hardly any preparation had been made for African self-rule. Although the Europeans had claimed to be bringing Commerce, Christianity, and Civilization to Africa, they had really come to profit themselves, and when their presence there ceased to be profitable they left as quickly as they could, with little regard for the future of the people they had exploited. As a result, the first generation after independence in Africa has had some hard lessons to learn. A hundred years of foreign occupation left the continent poorer and more chaotic than before, and the independence movements that so heroically freed the land were not always equipped to govern the new countries they had created.

After the initial excitement of freedom, the more than 50 countries of Africa have had to approach the problems of building their societies. They had at last achieved the goal expressed in Marcus Garvey's motto "Africa for the Africans," but they were still faced with the ancient challenges of the continent, as well as political, social, and economic problems that they had never had before the Europeans came. Some, like Kenya and Malawi, have progressed steadily, taking what was useful from the European examples and establishing relatively stable and prosperous societies under governments suited to their own national heritage. Others, like Angola, Nigeria, and Zaire, suffered civil wars as bloody as anything they experienced in freeing themselves. Still others, like Uganda and the Central African Republic, replaced their colonial masters with African tyrants who enslaved them worse than the Europeans had done. The result has often been social and political upheaval. In the last quarter century there have been 20 successful revolutions, and 70 leaders have been overthrown in 29 countries.

Social and political instability has often been the result of poverty. Political independence is only the first step toward real freedom. The next step is economic independence. Colonialism did little to equip the continent to develop and profit from its own resources. Even though European occupation created great economic growth, it left the former colonies in a state of dependence on the technology and the financial support of industrialized states without preparing them for self-sufficiency. Both Western Europe and the Communist countries took advantage of the new nations' needs, binding them economically and creating a relationship that has been called "neo-colonialism." Unprepared by education or experience to adjust to their new situations, the African nations have sometimes been guilty of overspending, excessive borrowing, inefficient investment, and corruption, all leading to still greater dependence on foreign capital to survive.

Not all of Africa's problems have been the result of its own failures. During the past quarter century, Africa has also suffered from problems beyond its control. The market for its principal exports, agricultural and mineral, has fluctuated with world conditions. When the price of chocolate declined in the 1960s, for example, the economy of Ghana, which depends largely on its production of cocoa, was shattered. Natural disasters have added to the problems of Africa; drought and famine have wrecked the economies of Ethiopia and Somalia since the

*Modern Johannesburg, South Africa.* (Courtesy South African Consulate General, New York)

*N'Debele woman decorating her home with a traditional design in Transvaal, South Africa.* (Courtesy South African Consulate General, New York)

late 1980s. Malnutrition and lack of sanitation resulting from these natural catastrophes have brought about epidemics of cholera, diphtheria, and yellow fever. Recently AIDS has also taken a deadly toll in many African countries.

But although the independence movements that finally freed the continent were often unable to establish secure and prosperous nations at first, Africa has had some notable successes since winning its freedom. Some countries have been torn apart by ethnic and regional conflict but have resolved their differences and emerged stronger. Zaire, for example, had a painful birth as the Republic of the Congo in 1960. Its first prime minister, Patrice Lumumba, was killed after his ouster in the country's first year of independence from Belgium, and the Congo dissolved into civil war as the copper-rich province of Katanga declared itself a separate nation. Outside support from the United Nations and Belgium was required to hold the country together

# MODERN AFRICAN ART

The visual arts of Africa are as varied as the continent's many cultures. Evolved from a wide range of traditions, the paintings and sculptures produced today show as much diversity as those of Europe and North America. However, the African cultural experience has been different from that of Europe, and the arts reflect that difference.

Africa has an exceptionally rich history of art, ranging back to the sophisticated cave drawings of 6000 B.C. and including the advanced painting and architecture of ancient Egypt and the bronze castings of medieval Benin. The broad artistic heritage of the continent includes every medium, technique, and style, and has had a major influence on such modern European artists as Pablo Picasso.

Folk art continues to be very much alive in contemporary African culture and to play an important part in daily life. Makonde wood carvings from Tanzania, Ashanti cloth from Ghana, and brass sculpture from Nigeria all still have important ceremonial uses. Their traditional forms and patterns have been maintained and have influenced much of modern African art. But besides the folk paintings and sculpture produced for ritual use or for sale to tourists, many original works of art have been produced during and since the colonial period in Africa. Some of them are the work of trained artists who have studied Western art techniques (usually under European teachers), and some are created by self-taught artists who employ their own methods and styles and work from their own imagination.

until General Joseph Mobutu, the head of the army, seized power in 1965. Renaming himself Mobutu Sese Seko (as he renamed the country Zaire), he instituted a strong one-man government that granted little personal liberty to the people. In 1990 Zaire took a large step toward democracy when Mobutu gave in to public protest and agreed to bring his 26 years of absolute rule to an end and share his power with an opposition leader.

Many university-level art schools offering classical training were opened during the 1950s and 1960s, and academics in Nigeria, Sudan, Ethiopia, Uganda, Ghana, and Senegal offer courses in all the techniques of Western art. But workshops that gave students materials and basic instructions on mixing paint and making prints, without training in European techniques or subjects, have also been in operation since the 1930s. Such schools exist in Nigeria, Zaire, Congo, and Zimbabwe and have produced an extraordinary body of original artists who have remained uninfluenced by Western styles. A few graduates of these schools, such as the Nigerian painter Ben Enmwonwu, have gone on to study formally in Europe or the United States and have earned international reputations for work that combines classical techniques with traditional African images. However, the best of even those artists who have acquired their training exclusively in Western-style schools have retained in their work some elements of the African culture in which they grew up. Ibrahim es Salahi, perhaps the best known of all contemporary African artists, reflects the formal education he received at the academy in his native Sudan but brings the unmistakable character of his Arabic background to his work.

Because of the great cultural diversity of the continent, no single "African style" of modern art has emerged, but certain characteristic features are to be found in the best of all its contemporary painting and sculpture. Not only does some trace of traditional design often remain, but there is also a vigor, exuberance, and freedom from conventional tradition that reflects the independent African spirit.

Nigeria too went through a bitter struggle among its different tribes and political factions when it first gained independence from England in 1960. After numerous political assassinations, a harsh military government was established. In 1967 an eastern province dominated by the Ibo tribe seceded as the independent nation of Biafra, and a civil war that cost thousands of lives followed. Peace was finally restored in 1970, the national government guaranteed equal protection and full political rights to all tribes, and Nigeria became one of the most unified and prosperous nations in Africa. It is now a leader in the Economic Community of West African States, a multinational body organized to promote cooperation and trade among its members and foreign countries.

Perhaps the most encouraging recent sign of progress in Africa has been the beginnings of equal treatment of the races in South Africa. After many years of fruitless African resistance to apartheid, the wall separating black and white in that country finally began to crumble in 1990 as president F. W. de Klerk brought about the repeal of the last major laws segregating the races. The government of South Africa has tentatively scheduled its first completely open election for April 27, 1994. On that date, black, white, and Coloured will vote for a 400-member assembly, its first post-apartheid parliament, ending more than 300 years of white rule. Though it is still not complete, the end of apartheid seems at long last to be in sight.

Economic independence, political stability, and social justice pres-ent many challenges. Africa must finish the job of freeing itself from foreign power by developing the resources that make it potentially the richest and most powerful continent in the world. Kwame Nkrumah spoke for all Africa at the United Nations when he recalled the days of "imperialism, exploitation, and degradation" and said, "These days are gone forever and now I . . . speak with the voice of freedom proclaiming to the world the dawn of a new era."

## CHAPTER 11 NOTES

p. 120     "Civilized or not civilized, . . ." Tom Mboya, speech at the All African People's Conference (AAPC), 1958, quoted in George M. Houser. *No One Can Stop the Rain* (New York: The Pilgrim Press, 1989), p. 363.

pp. 124–   "We did not 'lose' an Empire . . ." Iain Macleod, quoted in Martin
125        Meredith. *The First Dance of Freedom: Black Africa in the Postwar Era* (New York: Harper & Row, 1984), p. 132.

p. 132     "These days are gone forever . . ." Kwame Nkrumah, address to the General Assembly of the United Nations, New York, 1961, quoted in David Rooney. *Kwame Nkrumah* (New York: St. Martin's Press 1988), p. 181.

# INDEPENDENT NATIONS OF AFRICA

| Name | Former Name | Former Colonial Power | Date of Independence |
|---|---|---|---|
| **Algeria** | | France | 1962 |
| **Angola** | | Portugal | 1975 |
| **Benin** | Dahomey | France | 1960 |
| **Botswana** | Bechuanaland | Britain | 1966 |
| **Burkina Faso** | Upper Volta | France | 1960 |
| **Burundi** | Urundi | Germany; Belgium | 1962 |
| **Cameroon** | The Cameroons | Germany; France | 1960 |
| **Cape Verde Islands** | | Portugal | 1975 |
| **Central African Republic** | Ubangi-Shari | France | 1960 |
| **Chad** | | France | 1960 |
| **Comoro Islands** | | France | 1975 |
| **Congo** | Middle Congo | France | 1960 |

| Name | Former Name | Former Colonial Power | Date of Independence |
|---|---|---|---|
| **Djibouti** | French Somaliland | France | 1977 |
| **Egypt** | United Arab Republic (with Syria 1958–61) | Britain | 1922 |
| **Equatorial Guinea** | Spanish Guinea | Spain | 1968 |
| **Ethiopia** | | Italy (occupied, 1936–41) | |
| **Gabon** | | France | 1960 |
| **The Gambia** | Gambia | Britain | 1965 |
| **Ghana** | Gold Coast | Britain | 1957 |
| **Guinea** | French Guinea | France | 1958 |
| **Guinea-Bissau** | Portuguese Guinea | Portugal | 1974 |
| **Ivory Coast** | | France | 1960 |
| **Kenya** | | Britain | 1963 |
| **Lesotho** | Basutoland | Britain | 1966 |
| **Liberia** | | | 1847 |
| **Libya** | | Italy; Britain and France | 1951 |
| **Madagascar** | Malagasy Republic | France | 1960 |
| **Malawi** | Nyasaland | Britain | 1964 |
| **Mali** | French Sudan | Britain | 1960 |
| **Mauritania** | | France | 1960 |
| **Mauritius** | | Britain | 1968 |
| **Morocco** | | France and Spain | 1956 |
| **Mozambique** | Portuguese East Africa | Portugal | 1975 |

| Name | Former Name | Former Colonial Power | Date of Independence |
|---|---|---|---|
| Namibia | South-West Africa | Germany; South Africa | 1990 |
| Niger | | France | 1960 |
| Nigeria | | Britain | 1960 |
| Rwanda | Ruanda | Germany; Belgium | 1962 |
| São Tomé and Príncipe | | Portugal | 1975 |
| Senegal | | France | 1960 |
| Seychelles | | Britain | 1976 |
| Sierra Leone | | Britain | 1961 |
| Somalia | British and Italian Somaliland | Britain and Italy | 1960 |
| South Africa | | Britain | 1931 |
| Sudan | Anglo-Egyptian Sudan | Britain and Egypt | 1956 |
| Swaziland | | Britain | 1968 |
| Tanzania | Tanganyika and Zanzibar | Britain | 1964 |
| Togo | Togoland | Germany; France and Britain | 1960 |
| Tunisia | | France | 1956 |
| Uganda | | Britain | 1962 |
| Western Sahara (SADR) | Spanish Sahara | Spain | |
| Zaire | Belgian Congo | Belgium | 1960 |
| Zambia | Northern Rhodesia | Britain | 1964 |
| Zimbabwe | Southern Rhodesia | Britain | 1980 |

# CHRONOLOGY

332 B.C.   • Alexander of Macedon conquers Egypt.

168 B.C.   • Rome colonizes Egypt.

A.D. 700   • Arabs colonize East Africa and begin slave trade with Asia.

1441   • Portugal initiates slave trade with Europe.

1481   • Portuguese establish first settlement in present-day Ghana.

1482   • Portuguese colonize Angola.

1517   • Turkish Empire conquers Egypt.

1652   • Dutch establish settlement at Cape of Good Hope.

1787   • British found Sierra Leone Company to resettle freed slaves.

1795   • British occupy Cape Colony in present-day South Africa.

1822   • United States founds Liberia to resettle freed slaves.

1830   • French occupy Algeria.

1847   • Liberia is declared independent.

1868   • British declare Basutoland (now Lesotho) a protectorate.

1874   • British occupy Gold Coast (now Ghana).

1881 • French invade and establish protectorate in Tunisia.

1884 • Belgium's King Léopold establishes the Congo Free State.

• Germans occupy South-West Africa (now Namibia), Cameroons, and Togoland (now Togo).

1885 • Berlin Conference formally partitions Africa.

1889 • British and Egyptians establish joint rule in Sudan.

1890 • British declare Zanzibar (now part of Tanzania) and East Africa (now Kenya) protectorates.

• Germans occupy Tanganyika (now part of Tanzania).

1891 • British declare Nyasaland (now Malawi) and Bechuanaland (now Botswana) protectorates.

1893 • British declare Uganda a protectorate.

1894 • French occupy Dahomey (now Benin).

1895 • British declare British East Africa (now Kenya) a protectorate.

• French declare Madagascar a protectorate.

1896 • Italians invade Ethiopia but are defeated.

1902 • British defeat Dutch settlers in South Africa in the Boer War .

1908 • Congo Free State becomes a Belgian colony as the Belgian Congo.

1911 • Italians occupy Libya.

1912 • Italians and Arabs declare protectorates in Morocco.

1914 • British declare Egypt a protectorate.

1919 • League of Nations places former German colonies under the administration of Britain, France, Belgium, and South Africa.

1922 • Egypt becomes independent.

1931 • Union of South Africa becomes an independent member of the British Commonwealth.

1935 • Italians conquer Ethiopia.

1941 • Italians are driven out of Ethiopia.

1951 • Libya becomes independent.

  • Mau Mau rebellion begins in Kenya.

1954 • Algerian revolution begins.

1956 • Morocco, Tunisia, and Sudan become independent.

1957 • Gold Coast (now Ghana) becomes independent.

1958 • French colonies in West Africa are offered choice of independence or membership in the French Community.

  • French Guinea (now Guinea) becomes independent.

1960 • "The Year of Africa": 17 colonies become independent from France, Great Britain, and Belgium.

1961 • Sierra Leone and Tanganyika (now part of Tanzania) become independent.

  • Angolan revolution begins.

1962 • Algeria, Uganda, Ruanda (now Rwanda), and Urundi (now Burundi) become independent.

1963 • Kenya and Zanzibar (now part of Tanzania) become independent.

1964 • Nyasaland (now Malawi) and Northern Rhodesia (now Zambia) become independent.

1965 • The Gambia becomes independent.

1966 • Bechuanaland (now Botswana) and Basutoland (now Lesotho) become independent.

1968 • UN General Assembly formally terminates South Africa's mandate in South-West Africa, declaring its occupation there illegal.

  • Spanish Guinea (now Equatorial Guinea), Swaziland, and Mauritius become independent.

  • UN officially recognizes Namibia.

1974 • Guinea-Bissau becomes independent.

1975 • Angola, Cape Verde Islands, Comoros, Mozambique, and São Tomé and Príncipe, the last Portuguese colonies in Africa, become independent.

1976 • Seychelles become independent.

1977 • Djibouti, last French colony in Africa, becomes independent.

1980 • Rhodesia (now Zimbabwe), the last British colony in Africa, becomes independent.

1990 • Namibia, the last colony in Africa, becomes independent.

# FURTHER READING

## GENERAL HISTORIES

Davidson, Basil, *Africa: History of a Continent* (New York: Macmillan, 1972). Comprehensive overview of the continent from prehistoric times to the beginnings of the postcolonial period.

Du Bois, W. E. B., *The Souls of Black Folk* (Chicago: A.C. McClurg, 1903). Profound examination of the experience of the African people in history.

————, *Dusk of Dawn: An Essay Toward an Autobiography of a Race Concept* (New York: Harcourt Brace, 1940). Discussion of the meaning and influence of race in people's thought.

————, *The World and Africa* (New York: Viking, 1947). The place of Africa in world history ancient and modern.

Oliver, Roland and J. D. Fage, *A Short History of Africa*, sixth edition (London: Penguin Books, 1988). Balanced, wide-ranging summary.

Ungar, Sanford J., *Africa: The People and Politics of an Emerging Continent* (New York: Simon & Schuster, 1989). Up-to-date picture of contemporary Africa; emphasizes the political and economic history.

## COLONIALISM AND INDEPENDENCE

Fanon, Frantz, *A Dying Colonialism* (New York: Grove Press, 1961). Social and psychological study of colonialism and independence; a moving and influential work.

————, *The Wretched of the Earth* (New York: Grove Press, 1966). Classic revolutionary text arguing the need for violence in the struggle for liberation; now controversial.

Garvey, Marcus, *Philosophy and Opinions of Marcus Garvey*, two volumes, compiled by Amy Jacques-Garvey (New York: Universal Publishing House, 1923–26). Collection of Garvey's speeches and writings about African-American economic independence and the establishment of an African homeland.

Gibson, Richard, *African Liberation Movements: Contemporary Struggle Against White Minority Rule* (New York: Oxford University Press, 1972). Partisan examination of liberation struggles still taking place when the book was written, focusing on South Africa, Namibia, Zimbabwe, and the Portuguese colonies.

Grundy, Kenneth, *Guerrilla Struggle in Africa: An Analysis and Preview* (New York: Grossman, 1971). Military history of African independence battle; a little out of date but still exciting.

Hallett, Robin, *Africa Since 1875: A Modern History* (Ann Arbor, Mich.: University of Michigan Press, 1974). In-depth examination of the many strands of modern African history, sympathetically reported with interesting anecdotes.

Hodgkins, Thomas, *Nationalism in Colonial Africa* (New York: New York University Press, 1957). Examination of the rise of national sentiment in Africa and its influence on liberation movements.

Houser, George M. *No One Can Stop the Rain: Glimpses of Africa's Liberation Struggle* (New York: The Pilgrim Press, 1989). First-hand look at the battle with colonialism in some parts of Africa by a Methodist clergyman who observed it.

Luthuli, Albert, *Let My People Go* (New York: Prentice Hall, 1962). Nobel Peace Prize–winner's fight against racial discrimination in South Africa.

Mathabane, Mark, *Kaffir Boy: The True Story of a Black Youth's Coming of Age in Apartheid South Africa* (New York: Macmillan, 1990). Gripping personal account of modern-day life in South Africa.

Nkrumah, Kwame, *Africa Must Unite* (London: Panof, 1963). Passionate call for African unity by one of the continent's most important independence leaders.

Rotberg, Robert I. and Ali A. Mazrui, eds., *Protest and Power in Black Africa* (New York: Oxford University Press, 1976). Often exciting collection of articles describing African rebellions from early anti-conquest battles to postindependence revolutions.

Wallerstein, Immanuel, *Africa: The Politics of Independence* (New York: Vintage, 1961). Examination of the problems of postcolonial government; not always easy reading but informative.

Whitaker, Jennifer Seymour. *How Can Africa Survive?* (New York: Harper & Row, 1988). Respectful and insightful observation of contemporary Africa and its problems.

## FICTION

Achebe, Chinua, *Things Fall Apart* (New York: Astor-Honor, 1958). Funny and tragic tale of the tensions introduced into Nigerian society by the coming of the whites.

Gordimer, Nadine, *The Late Bourgeois World* (New York: Viking Penguin, 1983). Moving novel about personal relations between the races in South Africa.

Laye, Camara, *The African Child* (London: Fontana, 1955). Clear picture of traditional Guinean village life showing a stable society without European influence.

Paton, Alan, *Cry, the Beloved Country* (New York: Scribners, 1960). Gripping story of racial conflicts in South Africa and their impact on a family.

Soyinke, Wole, *Five Plays* (New York: Oxford University Press, 1967). Portrayal of social and political weaknesses in postindependence Nigeria by that country's leading dramatist.

Tutuola, Amos, *The Palm-Wine Drinkard* (New York: Grove Press, 1954). Jungle fantasy in the tradition of tribal folk tales.

## POETRY

Kennedy, Ellen Conroy, ed., *The Negritude Poets* (New York: Thunder's Mouth Press, 1989). Work by 27 poets of the Caribbean and Africa, with interesting introductions on each, translated from the French. Eloquent expressions of the love, passion, and rage of the African and African-American experience.

Moore, Gerald and Ulla Beier, eds., *Modern Poetry from Africa* (Baltimore: Penguin, 1966). Wide-ranging collection of contemporary African poetry by 13 French-African writers, with an excellent general introduction.

# INDEX

Boldface numbers indicate major topics.
*Italic* numbers indicate illustrations.
Numbers followed by "m" indicate maps.

neo-colonialism 128

*Néo-Destour* (ND) 93

Netherlands, the 9, 24, 80

Neto, Agostinho 117–118

Nigeria 24, 35, 67–68, 97, 127, 123, 131–132

Niger River 15

Nkrumah, Kwame xii, 39, 45–46, *64*, 64–66, 105, 106, 132

NNC *See* National Native Congress

North Africa 8, 10, 62

Northern Rhodesia 73–74, 121 *See also* Zambia

*Notes on a Return to the Native Land* (Aimé Césaire) 32, **56–57**

Nyasaland 53, 72–73 *See also* Malawi

Nyasaland African Congress (NAC) 72–73

Nyerere, Julius 68, 117

---

OAU *See* Organization of African Unity

Olduvai Gorge 1

Orange Free State 80

Organization of African Unity (OAU) 31, 43, 99, 113, **122–123**

Ovambo (people) 88

Ovamboland People's Congress *See* South-West African People's Organization (SWAPO)

"overseas territories" 26, 91–92, 98, 125–126 *See also* France, colonies

---

PAC *See* Pan-African Congress (political party)

Padmore, George 84

PAIGC *See Partido Africano da Indepêndencia de Guiné e Cabo Verde*

*Palm-Wine Drunkard, The* (Amos Tutuola) 124

Pan-African Association 37–38

Pan-African Conference of 1900 37–38, 82, 122

Pan-African Congress (1945) 66

Pan-African Congress (political party) 83, 86

Pan-Africanism 37–38

PARMEHUTU *See Parti d'Emancipation des Hutus* 109

Parti Démocratique de Guinée (PDG) 94

*Partido Africano da Indepnêdencia de Guiné e Cabo Verde* (PAIGC) 115, 116–117

passive resistance in South Africa 85

pass laws 82

paternalism, Belgian policy of 28

Paton, Alan 92, 125

PDG *See* Parti Démocratique de Guinée

People's Progressive Party (PPP) 75

*Philosophy and Opinions* (Marcus Garvey) 46

POLISARIO *See Frente Popular para la Liberación de Sekia el Hamra y Río de Oro*

Portugal
    colonial administration 16, 110–111, 114–115
    colonization 9, 16, 17, 23–24
    loss of colonies 110–111, 126, **113–119**
    resistance to 51

Portuguese East Africa (Mozambique) 23

Portuguese Guinea *See* Guinea–Bissau

PPP *See* People's Progressive Party

Príncipe *See* São Tomé and Príncipe

---

*Rassemblement Démocratique Africaine* (RDA) 92–93

RDA *See Rassemblement Democratique Africaine*

repatriation *See* Back-to-Africa movements

RF *See* Rhodesian Front

---